Better Homes and Gardens®

PAPER CRAFTS

BETTER HOMES AND GARDENS® BOOKS

Editor: Gerald M. Knox
Art Director: Ernest Shelton
Managing Editor: David A. Kirchner
Editorial Project Managers: Liz Anderson,
    James D. Blume, Marsha Jahns,
    Jennifer Speer Ramundt, Angela K. Renkoski

Crafts Editor: Sara Jane Treinen
Senior Crafts Editors: Beverly Rivers,
    Patricia Wilens
Associate Crafts Editor: Nancy Reames

Associate Art Directors: Neoma Thomas,
    Linda Ford Vermie, Randall Yontz
Assistant Art Directors: Lynda Haupert,
    Harijs Priekulis, Tom Wegner
Graphic Designers: Mary Schlueter Bendgen,
    Mike Burns, Brenda Lesch
Art Production: Director, John Berg
    Associate, Joe Heuer
    Office Manager, Michaela Lester

President, Book Group: Jeramy Lanigan
Vice President, Retail Marketing: Jamie L. Martin
Vice President, Administrative Services: Rick Rundall

BETTER HOMES AND GARDENS® MAGAZINE
President, Magazine Group: James A. Autry
Editorial Director: Doris Eby

MEREDITH CORPORATION OFFICERS
Chairman of the Executive Committee: E. T. Meredith III
Chairman of the Board: Robert A. Burnett
President: Jack D. Rehm

Paper Crafts
Editors: Sara Jane Treinen, Nancy Reames
Editorial Project Manager: Angela K. Renkoski
Graphic Designer: Linda Ford Vermie
Contributing Graphic Designer: Patricia Konecny
Electronic Text Processor: Paula Forest

Cover project: See page 20.

CONTENTS

Fun, Fast, and Easy
Paper Treasures _____ 4

If you're looking for quick ways to show off your crafting skills but at the same time create heirlooms that will be treasured for years, then the useful and decorative projects in this chapter will suit your fancy. Here are instructions for making Victorian bandboxes covered with wallpaper scraps, decorated purchased wooden jewelry boxes, and handmade picture frames trimmed with beautiful gift wrap papers. Other projects include a trio of Victorian silhouettes, a tray covered with a postage stamp collection, and a chest done up in old sheet music.

Favorite Techniques
For Gifts for Your Home _____ 18

Paper crafts enthusiasts who want to make exceptional gifts for friends or family, or decorate their homes with serendipitous items will find 10 great projects to choose from in this chapter. Included are two scherenschnitte designs, a standing three-dimensional Uncle Sam, two colonial flag designs, a papier-mâché tray and a duck decoy, and some quick and clever ways to "patch" up the kitchen.

A Birthday Party
Under the Big Tent _____ 36

A birthday party at the circus can happen any time of the year when you set the stage with the crafts in this chapter. Our circus party accessories include clown and animal wagon place mats, a cake that's decorated with sweets to look like a carousel, party favors, games, and several other colorful activities to keep the party performers busy and lively.

Paper Merriment
For Christmas _____ 60

Here's an assortment of festive trims to create a charming holiday ambience and gifts to delight your friends. A Santa ornament or standing decoration is fashioned from crepe paper. A wicker basket sleigh with cardboard reindeer makes a delightful table centerpiece. You'll send one-of-a-kind holiday greetings when you make either the trumpeting angel or the cross-stitched cards. And there are some wonderful scherenschnitte designs that can be cut for tree trims, tabletop decorating, or framing.

Acknowledgments _____ 80

PAPER TREASURES

♦♦♦

Decorative, versatile, and inexpensive, paper can be used to create an amazing array of beautiful and useful items. Not only is paper available in an infinite variety of pretty colors, patterns, weights, and textures, but paper also can be crafted in many different ways. In this chapter—and throughout this book—you'll discover the number of projects you can make with paper is limited only by your imagination.

Romantic and old-fashioned, the family silhouettes *left* and *opposite* will surely delight everyone with a fancy for Victorian times. Crafted in much the same way as silhouettes of the past would have been, each figure is clothed in the costumes of the early Victorian era.

You can make each paper portrait from a single sheet of black-coated paper, available at art and crafts stores. Frame the silhouettes in a suitably old-fashioned frame.

You also can cut shadow pictures of your own family members. First, take profile photographs and have them enlarged to 8x10-inch pictures. Using tracing paper, trace the outlines of the figures, then transfer the portraits to silhouette paper. Refer to the instructions on page 12 for cutting the silhouettes.

With paper too pretty to toss out, you can create charming, old-fashioned accents, like these Victorian-style bandboxes, for your home. Covered with wallpaper scraps and ordinary gift wrap, these beautiful boxes provide a special place to store all your trinkets and treasures.

Begin by making a basic box, using either artist's mat board or chipboard, depending on the shape you want. Assemble the box and matching lid, and secure with packing tape. Then cover the completed box with the paper of your choice.

Or, select a fancy fabric—satin, moiré, or chintz—as a substitute for the paper. The instructions include directions for making and covering boxes in oval, round, square, and hexagonal shapes.

PAPER TREASURES

The dazzling array of beautiful wrapping papers available today invite a much more imaginative use than the simple packaging of presents. With such a proliferation of patterns—from pretty florals to faux finishes—you're sure to find a paper to spark your imagination and inspire you to create exquisite keepsakes.

Covered with pieces of flowery gift wrap and lined with synthetic suede, the miniature chest and jewelry boxes, *right* and *opposite,* are unpainted pieces easily purchased at most crafts and hobby shops.

Paint the chest a rosy hue before applying paper. Or, choose a color that coordinates with your decor or the wrapping paper you plan to use. Designed to display dear-to-the-heart photos and mementos, the elegant pair of picture frames *opposite* will surely win a place of prominence in your home. A single roll of wrapping paper—or less—is all you'll need to make either of these lovely frames.

Both frames are fashioned from two pieces of mat board covered with gift wrap. To decorate the front of the large frame, roll tiny tubes of paper and glue in place. The small frame features a diamond design created by applying paper strips around the picture opening.

Make the most of a favorite collection by putting it on permanent display. An ever-growing cache of postage stamps was the inspiration for the tray *opposite.*

To make a distinctive stamp tray of your own, simply glue stamps in a random pattern to the top and bottom of a purchased plate or tray. Make the tray as we did, using a variety of stamps. Or, design a tray with a theme by choosing only Christmas stamps or those with a floral motif.

Play up an interest in music when you create a special place to stash the accessories for your hobby. The harmonious cupboard *above* is "papered" with pages of old sheet music. Wallpaper paste keeps the pages in place, and polyurethane varnish seals the surface.

Whatever your interest or hobby, you can easily "paper" a piece of unfinished furniture. Use a book of illustrated nursery rhymes to finish a toy or blanket chest for a baby's room. Or, cover a box for garden tools with empty seed packages or the pages from several seed catalogs. Pages from a book with botanical prints would make a lovely chest for the master bedroom.

PAPER TREASURES

Early Victorian Family Silhouettes

Shown on pages 4 and 5.

Finished size of the couple is 4¼x7¼ inches tall; the young boy is 1½x4¾ inches tall; the little girl is 2½x4⅞ inches tall.

MATERIALS

8½x11-inch thin, black, coated paper stock, available at art and crafts stores
Tracing paper
Graphite paper, available at art and crafts stores
Mat board, white or color of your choice
Stapler
Sharp 4-inch embroidery scissors or manicure scissors
White glue

INSTRUCTIONS

Trace one of the silhouette patterns, *right* and *opposite,* onto tracing paper. To keep the pattern from slipping, staple together the pattern, the graphite paper (graphite side down), and the black coated paper (black side facing down).

With a sharp pencil, draw on top of the tracing paper. For proper registration, be careful to go over every line only once. Remove staples and separate the papers.

In order to have a larger area of paper to grasp while cutting, begin to cut the inside areas of the silhouettes first. Then cut along the outside edges.

Always cut with the tips of the scissors, completely closing the tips at the end of each snip.

MOUNTING: Use small smears of white glue to mount the silhouettes onto the mat board. Glass will hold the silhouettes flat. If you use raised mats around the silhouettes, you need to completely glue the back of the silhouettes using a spray adhesive to mount silhouettes to the backings. Frame silhouettes as desired.

EARLY VICTORIAN FAMILY SILHOUETTES
Full-Size Patterns

Wallpaper Bandboxes

Shown on pages 6 and 7.

The boxes shown are in various sizes. See "Note" under the instructions *below*.

MATERIALS
30x40-inch sheet of single-weight chipboard for curved boxes; mat board for straight-sided boxes (dimensions of mat board are determined by size of box)
Wallpaper scraps
Wallpaper wheat paste
Wrapping paper
White crafts glue for attaching wrapping paper
Rice paper (optional, to cover wrapping paper)
Acrylic matte medium, for use with rice paper
1½-inch-wide package sealing tape
Straightedge or ruler
Utility knife, scissors, pencil
Protractor to make hexagon
String and 2 pushpins to make oval shape
½-inch-wide and 1-inch-wide soft brushes
White latex primer

INSTRUCTIONS
Note: The following directions will work for a box of any size. First determine the height and the dimensions of the top and bottom of the box style you wish to make.

To make a hexagonal box
To make the box bottom, refer to the diagram at *far right.* Use the straightedge to draw a horizon line and an intersecting line at right angles on the mat board.

Place protractor on horizon line at the intersection and make marks at 60 and 120 degrees. Draw lines through marks and horizon line at intersection. Turn board around and repeat markings on the opposite side. Connect horizon line and degree lines at equal distances from point of intersection to get the hexagon shape.

EARLY VICTORIAN FAMILY SILHOUETTES
Full-Size Patterns

When you extend the horizon line and 60- and 120-degree lines, you can change the size of the perimeter of the box. Use a utility knife to cut hexagon from mat board.

For sides of the box, cut a rectangle from mat board to match these dimensions. Draw lines atop the mat board to mark the six sides. Place the metal straightedge atop these lines, one at a time, and score the sides with utility knife. Don't cut all the way through the mat board. Fold the mat board on scored lines and attach sides to the bottom of the box with packing tape. Tape the side seam closed and reinforce scored lines with packing tape.

Follow instructions for making box bottom to make the top of the lid, except make lid approximately ⅛ inch larger than the bottom. Make the sides of lid the same as the box sides, except cut the height of the sides to match the lid size that you want. Tape sides to top. Test the fit of the lid. Keep in mind that the paper covering the box will add thickness to the box and lid.

Seal the box inside and out with primer and let dry.

continued

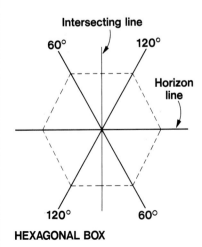

HEXAGONAL BOX

To make an oval box

To make the box bottom, refer to the diagram *below*. Pin the ends of a string at any two focal points on the chipboard. The length of the string must be about a third longer than the distance between the two focal points. Draw a line between the two points as shown by the horizontal line on the diagram.

Keeping the pencil perpendicular to the chipboard, push the pencil between the two focal points, keeping the pencil upright and snug against the string. Draw half of the oval. Then lift the pencil and move the string to the opposite side of the pins and draw the second half of the oval. Cut out the marked oval from the chipboard.

For the sides, determine the height and perimeter of the oval plus 1 inch for an overlap, and mark these measurements on the chipboard. To determine the perimeter, measure around the base of the cut oval with a string. Cut out the sides. Put one-half of the tape along one long edge of the side rectangle. Press remaining half of the tape along the box bottom, clipping curves as you fasten the sides. Tape side-seam overlap.

Follow the instructions for the box bottom to make the lid, except cut the lid approximately ⅛ inch larger than the bottom oval. Cut the lid side to fit the top, making the sides of the lid to correspond with the finished size of the lid.

Seal the boxes with primer inside and out; let dry.

For the square and round boxes

To make a square box, draw a square for the box bottom and

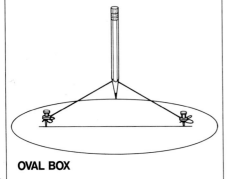

OVAL BOX

make the lid ⅛ inch larger all around. Follow the instructions for the hexagon box on page 13 to make the sides, except score four lines instead of six.

For a round box, use a circular object to draw around for box bottom. Make the lid ⅛ inch larger.

Seal the boxes with primer inside and out; let dry.

WALLPAPERING: Measure and cut wallpaper for the side of the box. Add 1 inch for overlap at bottom of box and 2 inches for overlap along top of box sides. For the lid, cut the paper the finished size of the distance around the sides, plus the overlap.

Mix the wallpaper paste following the manufacturer's instructions. Apply paste to wallpaper, and paste paper to sides of box. Clip curves of overlap and fold 1 inch over the bottom. Clip curves of 2-inch overlap and fold to inside of box top. Repeat for the sides of the lid.

Draw around the lid and the bottom on the paper. Cut paper ¼ inch inside the drawn lines. Test-fit the paper on bottom and top; trim if needed. Brush paste on paper. Apply paper to bottom and lid top.

To cover the box with wrapping paper follow the same steps as *above,* except use white crafts glue diluted with enough water to glue paper to box.

Rice paper adds another texture and makes the colors of the paper more subtle. We used rice paper atop wrapping paper on the oval box shown in the photograph on page 6. To use rice paper, measure and cut the pieces (the same dimensions as the wrapping paper) to fit over the box. Brush the diluted matte medium over rice paper and press the rice paper atop the paper-covered box; let dry.

To add an optional cord handle, shown on the round box on page 7, attach purchased grommets according to the manufacturer's instructions. Thread cording through the holes. Determine the length of the cord you desire, and tie an overhand knot in the cord on the inside of box.

Wrapping-Paper Picture Frames

Shown on page 9.

The large frame is 9x11 inches; small frame is 6½x7½ inches.

MATERIALS
For both frames
One or more packages wrapping paper in colors of your choice
Rubber cement and white crafts glue
Masking tape
Crafts knife
Awl
For the large frame
Two 9x11-inch pieces of mat board or chipboard
One 9x11-inch piece of foam-core board
7 inches of ⅜-inch-wide grosgrain ribbon to match paper
One 12-inch-long, ¼-inch-diameter wooden dowel
One 4½x8-inch sheet of 1/16-inch acrylic plastic
For the small frame
Two 6½x7½-inch pieces of mat board or chipboard
One 6½x7½-inch piece of foam-core board
One 3½x5½-inch sheet of 1/16-inch acrylic plastic

INSTRUCTIONS
For the large frame
Set one of the two pieces of mat board aside to use as backing board. Cut and remove a 4x6-inch window from the center of the other board to make the front of the frame.

From the wrapping paper, cut a 10x12-inch rectangle. Cover the back of the wrapping paper with rubber cement, and center it atop the frame front, gluing the surfaces together.

For the window opening, diagonally cut the paper from corner to corner, making an "X" cut. Fold the excess paper to the back of the frame and glue. Fold back ½-inch outer edge of wrapping paper and glue to back of frame. Set this piece aside.

To make the spacers (which separate the front of the frame from its backing to allow for placement of acrylic plastic sheet) for the backing board, cut one 2¼x9-inch foam-core strip, and referring to Diagram A, *far right,* glue this strip across one short edge of backing (bottom of frame). Cut two foam-core strips, *each* 2¼x8¾ inches, and glue one to each side of the backing.

Cut one 11x13-inch piece of wrapping paper. Center the paper on the backing atop the side that does not have the spacers, and fold the edges of paper over the three sides with the foam-core strips and glue in place. Referring to Diagram B, *far right,* cut the folded edge of the paper along the inside edge of the foam-core strips (marked in blue on diagram), and glue paper down to the board and strips.

With the awl, punch a hole in the center of the backing, 2 inches up from the bottom edge. Push one end of the ribbon through the hole to the wrong side. Fasten the end of the ribbon to the board with glue. Put tape over the end of the ribbon to give it extra strength.

Glue the backing board to the back of the frame.

Cut the hinged table support from foam-core board using the pattern on page 16. To create the hinge, score board along dashed line indicated on the pattern; bend the hinged portion back. Cover non-scored side of hinge with tape for reinforcement.

Cut the wrapping paper ½ inch larger than the support. Lay the support on the center of the paper, scored side up, and glue with the rubber cement, pulling paper edges around foam-core board. Cut another piece of paper slightly smaller than the inside dimension of the support, and glue to back side of the longer portion of the support.

Punch a hole in the center of the support 2 inches up from the bottom edge. Pull the ribbon on back of the frame backing board through the hole to the back of the support. Lay the support

piece flat against the back, lining up the bottom edge with bottom edge of the frame. Using white glue, glue the hinged portion only to back of backing board. Allow to dry thoroughly. When dry, position the hinged support so the frame will stand.

Adjust the length of ribbon so frame stands correctly; trim ribbon, leaving extra 2 inches. Tie a knot in the ribbon 1 inch from end. Push the ribbon end back through the hole to the back side of support. Trim off all but ½ inch of ribbon and glue to the back side of support.

To decorate the frame, cut 32 squares, 8½ inches each, of wrapping paper. Roll each into a tube by rolling paper around the dowel. Glue the ends with rubber cement and remove the dowel.

Use white glue to glue tubes to front of frame. Begin by gluing a tube at the top and one at the bottom. Then glue tubes on each side of the frame. Progress from the outside edges to the inside. Measure each tube as you work, and cut off the excess with the crafts knife. To do this neatly, insert the dowel into the end of each tube and use it as a firm surface for the knife to cut against. Repeat for the other end. Our frame has eight rows of tubes on each side.

To create the triangular pattern, cut 16 small triangles and 16 large triangles from a contrasting or complementary color of wrapping paper using the pattern on page 16. Glue the small triangle atop the larger triangle (right sides will face up, creating 16 triangles).

Referring to the photo on page 9, fasten four triangles to each side of the frame as follows: glue one triangle in front of the fourth row of tubes, two in front of the fifth, and one in front of the sixth row. Position the points outward.

Slip the acrylic plastic sheet through the slot at the top of the frame.

For the small frame

Set aside one of the 6½x7½-inch pieces of mat board. Center and cut out a 3x4-inch window from the other piece of mat board.

Cut out an 8½x9½-inch piece of wrapping paper. Center the mat board and use rubber cement to glue it to the wrong side of the wrapping paper.

For the window, cut the paper from corner to corner, making an "X" cut. Fold the excess paper to the back of the frame and glue in place. Fold back ½-inch outer edge of wrapping paper and glue to back of frame. Measure and mark the center of each outside edge.

Cut four 2x9-inch strips and four 2x8-inch strips of wrapping paper. Fold over ½ inch of the long side of *each* strip of wrapping paper to meet in the center back.

Lay one 9-inch-long strip diagonally across one corner of the frame, and line up the edge of the
continued

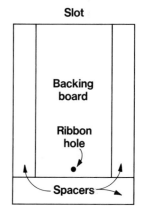

DIAGRAM A

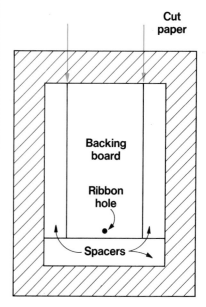

DIAGRAM B

strip with the center marks made on one of the frame sides. Glue in place. Fold excess portion of the strip to the back of frame, and glue. Repeat for the remaining three corners. Take four remaining 8-inch lengths and overlap the first strips on the inside edge. Glue these strips in place and finish in same manner.

To make the backing board, cut a 6½x7½-inch piece of mat board. For the spacers (which separate the front of the frame from its backing to allow for placement of acrylic plastic sheet), cut one 6½x1½-inch foam-core strip. Referring to Diagram A on page 15, glue this strip across one short edge of backing (bottom of frame). Cut two foam-core strips, *each* 1½x6 inches, and glue one to *each* side of the frame backing.

Referring to Diagram B on page 15, cut one 8½x9½-inch piece of wrapping paper. Center the paper on the backing atop the side that does not have the spacers, and fold the edges of paper over the three sides with the foam-core strips, and glue. Along the top edge, cut the folded edge of the paper along the inside edge of the foam-core strips, and glue paper down to the board and strips.

With the awl, punch a hole in the center of the backing, 1⅝ inches up from the bottom edge. Push one end of the ribbon through the hole to the wrong side. Fasten the end of the ribbon to the board with glue. Put tape over the end of the ribbon to give it extra strength.

Glue the backing board to the back of the frame.

Cut the hinged table support from foam-core board using the pattern *below*. To create the hinge in the support, score the board along the line indicated on the pattern; bend the hinged portion back. Cover the non-scored side of the hinge with tape for reinforcement.

Cut wrapping paper ½ inch larger all around than the support. Lay the support on the center of the paper, scored side up, and glue with the rubber cement, pulling paper edges around foam-core board. Cut another piece of paper slightly smaller than the inside dimension of the hinged support; glue to the back side of the longer portion of the support.

Punch a hole in the center of the support 1⅝ inches up from the bottom edge. Pull the ribbon on back of the frame backing board through the hole to the back of the support. Lay the support piece flat against the back, lining up the bottom edge with bottom edge of the frame. Using white glue, glue the hinged portion only to the back of backing board. Allow to dry thoroughly. When dry, position the hinged support so the frame will stand.

Adjust the length of ribbon so frame stands correctly; trim ribbon, leaving extra 2 inches. Tie a knot in the ribbon 1 inch from end. Push the ribbon end back through the hole to the back side of support. Trim off all but ½ inch of ribbon, and glue to the back side of support.

Insert the piece of thin acrylic plastic sheet through the slot at the top of the frame.

Wrapping-Paper Jewelry Boxes And Chest

Shown on pages 8 and 9.

Sizes of boxes shown are as follows: The smaller box is 4¾x3¾x1¾ inches, and the larger box is 5½x4¾x2¼ inches. Chest is 10x10¼x4¾ inches.

MATERIALS
Unfinished wood box
Floral wrapping paper
Rice paper
Extra-tacky crafts glue
Matte polymer medium
Clear acrylic sealer
Tape measure; scissors
Metal ruler; crafts knife
Rubber brayer (found in art and crafts stores)
Waxed paper
Synthetic suede for the box lining or drawer linings

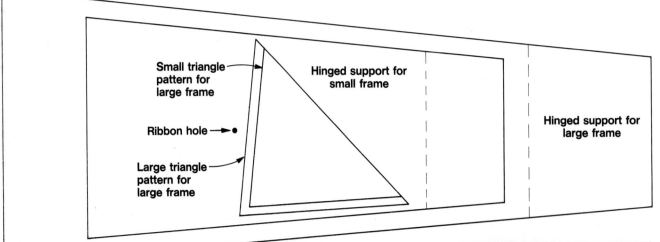

Small triangle pattern for large frame

Hinged support for small frame

Ribbon hole

Large triangle pattern for large frame

Hinged support for large frame

WRAPPING-PAPER PICTURE FRAMES
Full-Size Patterns

Materials for the chest
Unfinished five-drawer wooden chest
Rose-colored acrylic paint
Off-white acrylic paint
One ½-inch flat brush
Soft cloth

INSTRUCTIONS

Note: For best success with this project, allow the glue to dry thoroughly between each step.

BOX PREPARATION: Remove all of the metal hardware, drawer knobs, and lids from the boxes or chest you plan to cover.

Prime all wood surfaces with a clear acrylic sealer. This will ensure a good bond between the paper, glue, and box.

FOR THE CHEST: Use the ½-inch flat brush to apply the rose paint to the outside edges of the chest and the separations between the drawers. Also paint the wooden drawer knobs (if any) that had been removed. Let dry.

Make a mixture of one-half off-white paint with one-half water. Brush the diluted off-white paint mixture onto the dry rose paint. Use the cloth to gently wipe off paint to create a softer look. Let dry.

Use the metal ruler and crafts knife to cut wrapping paper to fit the areas you would like covered (the fronts of drawers, the sides and top of the chest). Do not cover the spaces around the drawers. See the photograph on page 8 for details.

Use the extra-tacky crafts glue to attach the paper to the chest.

FOR SMALL BOXES: Use the ruler to measure the outside dimensions of your box.

Cut one piece of wrapping paper to cover the front, bottom, and back of the bottom half of the box. Cut 2 rectangular pieces of paper to cover the sides of the bottom half of the box. Use the tacky crafts glue to attach the paper to the box. Let dry thoroughly.

Measure and cut a narrow piece of paper to fit inside lip of box. Use the tacky crafts glue to attach paper to the box lip.

Measure, cut paper, and cover the box lid same as for the bottom of the box.

When both box halves are completely dry, use scissors to trim excess paper from the edges.

TO ADD RICE PAPER: Use the same box measurements and cut rice paper to cover all of the wrapping paper (including the inner box lip on small boxes).

Make a mixture of half matte polymer medium to same amount of water. Lay rice paper over the box and carefully brush the mixture over the rice paper. The rice paper is very easily torn at this point. Cover with a piece of waxed paper and roll the brayer on top of the waxed paper to smooth the rice paper underneath. Remove the waxed paper.

For the small boxes, dry both of the box halves upside down on top of cans.

Do not try to move the box or chest until it is thoroughly dry. Trim the rice paper from the box edges.

To secure the rice paper add a couple of coats of the matte polymer medium mixture. Allow to dry thoroughly.

TO LINE BOXES OR DRAWERS: Use a tape measure to find the width, length, and depth of the insides of the box or drawer. Cut one piece of synthetic suede to fit across the bottom and depth of two opposite sides. Cut two pieces of suede to line the other two opposite sides of the bottom of box (and each drawer).

Test the fit of the synthetic suede liner in the inside of the box or drawer before gluing. Trim or recut if necessary. Use the tacky crafts glue to attach the suede to the drawers or to the inside of the box.

Repeat the lining steps above to line lid.

Locate the original holes where the hardware was and attach the hardware to the finished pieces. Use glue to hold hardware onto box if necessary.

Postage Stamp Tray

Shown on page 10.

MATERIALS
Assorted postage stamps
One purchased plastic, wood, or metal plate or tray, size of your choice
Spray acrylic primer
Crafts glue
Spray polyurethane varnish

INSTRUCTIONS
Apply the spray primer to the tray or plate of your choice. Spray one side; let dry. Spray the other side; let dry.

Using small amounts of crafts glue, affix stamps to the tray in a random pattern. Cover the entire tray, top and bottom. Let the glue dry thoroughly.

Seal the tray with the polyurethane varnish, one side at a time; let dry. Spray the other side. Repeat the spraying one more time.

Sheet-Music Cupboard

Shown on page 11.

MATERIALS
Unfinished cupboard
One book of sheet music
Wall-covering adhesive
Sandpaper
Wood filler
Spray polyurethane varnish

INSTRUCTIONS
Remove any door pulls, hardware, or moldings from the cupboard. Fill holes, and sand all the surfaces.

Trim sheet music evenly. Using the wall-covering adhesive, affix sheet music randomly across surface. Trim away any of the sheet music that does not fit on the wood surfaces.

When dry, seal surfaces twice with polyurethane varnish spray. Allow varnish to dry between each application.

FAVORITE TECHNIQUES

FOR GIFTS
FOR YOUR HOME

There are many ways you can work with paper to produce a variety of accessories for your home. Perhaps it's this amazing versatility that makes paper one of the most popular crafts materials. In this section, we offer a sampling of such classic techniques as papier-mâché and decoupage.

True American spirit and an appreciation for the past inspired the two paper flags *below* and *opposite*. Make these ingenious decorations with brown paper grocery bags that have been dampened. Then crumple, tear, tatter, and paint the bags.

The Uncle Sam figure *below* is crafted from paper plates and empty paper-towel tubes. Instant papier-mâché forms the hair and beard. Acrylic paint and antiquing stain complete this patriotic figure.

Instructions begin on page 26.

Scherenschnitte, a paper-cutting technique made popular by the Pennsylvania Dutch in the late 18th and 19th centuries, produces intricate paper designs as delicate and lovely as lace. Traditionally, this method of paper work was used to create keepsakes celebrating life's special moments, such as a marriage or the birth of a child. Often, these lacy mementos were painted and inscribed with sentimental sayings.

Th_ese cut-paper keepsakes are patterned after classic scherenschnitte designs. Heart and flower motifs detail the designs, and inscriptions written with a crow-quill pen and ink add old-fashioned charm.

Both the rocking horse design, *opposite,* and the anniversary design, *above,* are cut from lightweight paper. Once the cutting is complete, dab on a delicate stain of instant coffee and water to "antique" the design.

FAVORITE TECHNIQUES

With a stack of old newspapers and a pot of wallpaper paste, you can create such decorative items as the papier-mâché fish tray *above* and the duck decoy *opposite.*

Build a wire frame and cover it with torn newspapers and paste.

Allow the shape to dry completely. Then, using acrylic paints and your imagination, paint the shape to suit your home decor. To waterproof the tray for serving food, spray on a varnish or acrylic sealer.

Country quilt designs are a snap to "piece" with these cut-and-paste patchwork projects. We used the same technique to top the timeworn table *above* and *opposite,* and the plain round wooden tray, *opposite.* You can use it on similar items or any flat wood surface.

Choose a quilt design and pick any number of wallpaper scraps to decorate your wooden "quilt." Then, cut and glue wallpaper scraps to a primed wooden object.

Create a custom look for your walls with inexpensive, easy-to-install paper wall tiles. Squares of black and white adhesive-backed paper make up the wall treatment *opposite.* Grouting is simply the underlying wall paint showing through. Tiles are easily repositioned if they are incorrectly placed. Just peel them off and stick them down again as many times as necessary.

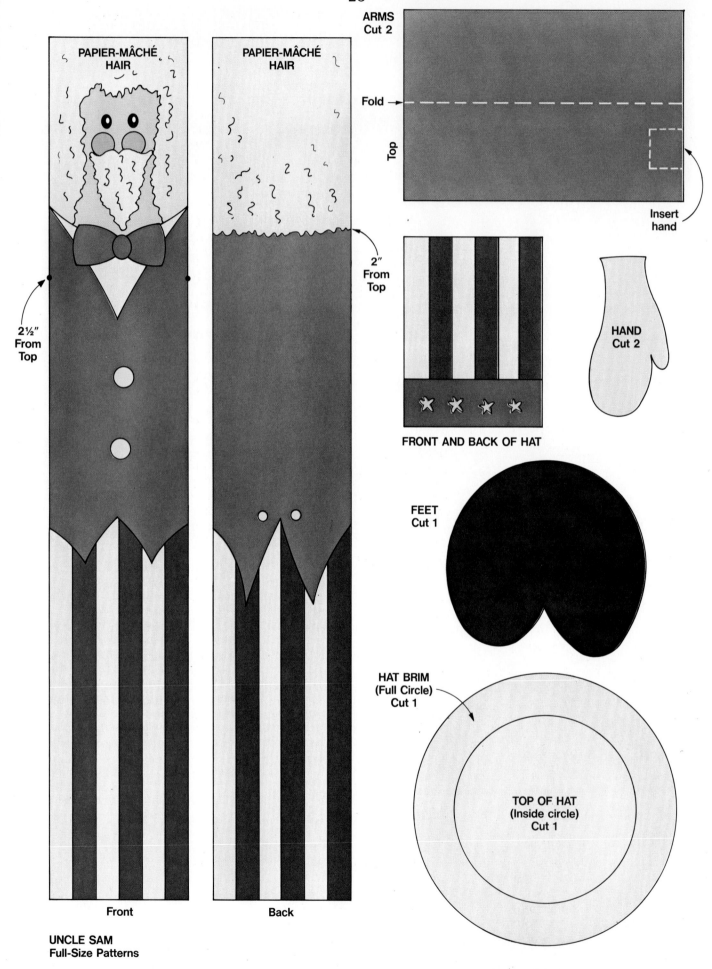

PAPIER-MÂCHÉ HAIR

PAPIER-MÂCHÉ HAIR

2½" From Top

Front

Back

UNCLE SAM
Full-Size Patterns

ARMS Cut 2

Fold →

Top

Insert hand

2" From Top

HAND Cut 2

FRONT AND BACK OF HAT

FEET Cut 1

HAT BRIM (Full Circle) Cut 1

TOP OF HAT (Inside circle) Cut 1

Uncle Sam Decoration

Shown on page 18.

Uncle Sam stands 11 inches tall.

MATERIALS
Two 11-inch-long empty paper
    towel tubes
6 paper plates
White, deep red, dark blue,
    flesh-color, black, and pink
    acrylic paints
Clear yellow tacky glue found in
    crafts stores
Gesso
Wood glue
Two ¾-inch paper brads
Instant papier-mâché (can be
    found in crafts stores)
One 1¼-inch-wide and one fine
    paintbrush
Scissors
Ruler
Pencil
Ice pick
Crafts knife
Water-base antique stain
Clear spray acrylic sealer
4–6 clothespins

INSTRUCTIONS
Note: Proper drying after *each*
step is essential for the success of
this project.
    For the body and the hat, use
the crafts knife to cut one empty
cardboard paper towel tube into
one 9-inch length for the body
and one 2-inch length for the hat.
    Stack three paper plates and
glue them together using wood
glue. Glue remaining three plates
together. Allow to dry thoroughly.
    Referring to the patterns, *oppo-
site,* trace the hand, feet, top of
hat, and hat brim onto tracing paper; cut out the patterns. Cut
these pieces from the glued paper
plates.
    For the arms, cut the second
towel tube into two 3-inch
lengths. Flatten these two pieces.
Trace the arm pattern, *opposite,
top right,* onto tracing paper; cut
out two arms from the flattened
tubes. Fold the arm pieces in half

so they are 1 inch wide. To complete one arm and hand segment,
place wrist of hand inside arm
where marked on the pattern,
and glue the arm together. Make
the second arm. Hold each arm
together with clothespins until
the glue dries. Round off the top
of each arm.
    Apply a coat of the clear yellow
tacky glue to all surfaces of the
pieces, including the paper towel
tubes. Allow at least 2 hours to
dry thoroughly.
    When all pieces are completely
dry, apply a coat of gesso to all
surfaces. As the pieces dry, they
will crack to give the illusion of
being old and weathered. When
the gesso layer is dry, use the
acrylic paints to color the pieces,
referring to the diagrams, *opposite,* for color placements. Use the
uncut edge of the paper tube at
the bottom to give the piece great-
er stability for standing. Allow the
paint to dry thoroughly.
    For the arm attachments on the
body, measure 2½ inches down
from the top of the 9-inch tube,
and punch one hole from the
shoulder position on each side
using the ice pick. Measure ½
inch down from the curve at the
top of each arm, and punch a hole
in the center. Making sure the
thumbs are facing forward, attach arms to the body by insert-
ing a paper brad through each
hole. Place your finger inside the
top of the body tube and open the
brads.
    Use wood glue to glue the hat
brim, sides, and top together.
Trim the top of the hat if it hangs
over the sides after the glue is dry.
    Glue the hat to the top of the 9-
inch tube. Mix instant papier-mâché according to manufacturer's
instructions, and apply hair and
beard as shown on the drawing,
opposite, far left, and referring to
the photograph on page 18. Allow
several hours for hair and beard
to dry. Paint white.
    Roll up some of the leftover por-
tions of the paper plates, and dip
them into some wood glue. Insert
these into the bottom of the tube
to provide extra weight for support and stability.

Use wood glue to attach the feet
to the bottom of the tube.
    Use the water-base antique
stain to antique Uncle Sam to the
desired color. Apply 5 or 6 coats of
clear acrylic sealer. Allow each
coat of the sealer to dry thoroughly before applying the next coat.

Americana Heart

Shown on page 18.

Finished heart is 11x9¾ inches.

MATERIALS
3 to 4 brown paper grocery bags
Wood glue
Creative paper twist in natural
    color (can be purchased in
    crafts stores)
White, deep red, and dark blue
    acrylic paint
Water-base antique stain
Clear spray acrylic sealer (matte
    finish or gloss, depending
    upon desired look)
One 20-inch length of ¼-inch-
    diameter jute twine
Scissors; ice pick
Ruler
Fine and ¾-inch-wide
    paintbrushes

INSTRUCTIONS
    Trace large and small heart pat-
terns on page 28 onto tracing paper; cut out patterns. Cut 2 large
hearts and 3 small hearts from
brown paper grocery bags. Crumple the paper hearts to achieve an
aged, worn effect.
    Dampen the edges of the 2 large
hearts with water. Fold hearts in
half along the center fold line, and
tear away small pieces around the
edges for a tattered, ragged look.
(Hearts should be 9¾ inches long
after being tattered).
    Make a mixture of two parts
wood glue to one part water. Dip 1
large heart into the mixture,
squeeze out excess liquid, and lay
flat on a plastic surface.

continued

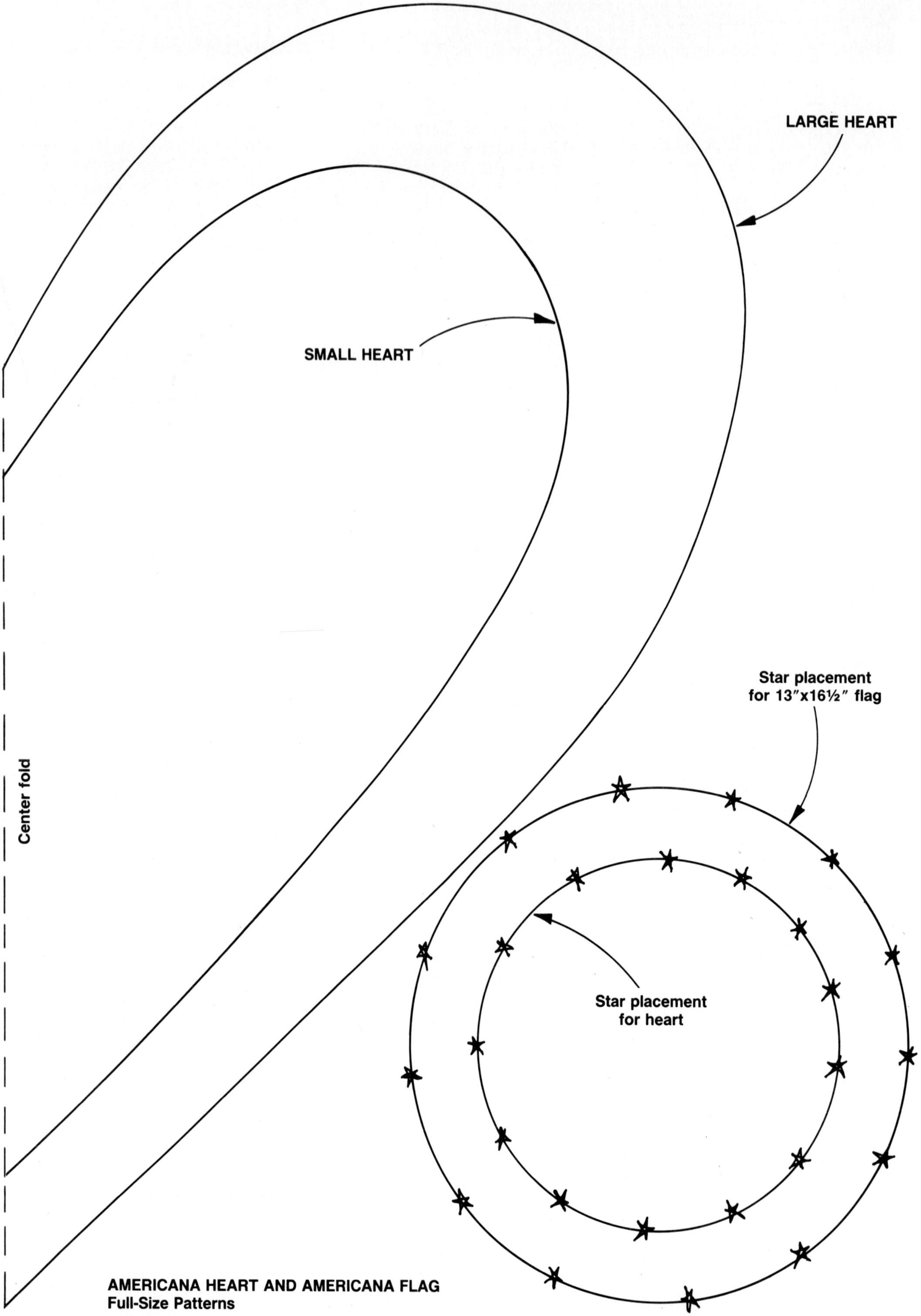

28

LARGE HEART

SMALL HEART

Center fold

Star placement
for 13"x16½" flag

Star placement
for heart

AMERICANA HEART AND AMERICANA FLAG
Full-Size Patterns

Dip each of the small hearts into the glue mixture, squeeze out excess liquid, and layer over the center of the large heart.

Dip the remaining large heart into the glue mixture, and place on top of the other hearts, sandwiching the 3 small hearts between the 2 large hearts.

Allow the heart to dry. Then paint both sides with the white acrylic paint; let dry. Use a soft cloth to antique the white heart with the antique stain.

Measure and, using the pencil, lightly mark lines for thirteen, ¾-inch-wide stripes. The first stripe through the seventh will cover only the upper right portion of the heart, so measure from the center fold to the right edge. The eighth stripe through the 13th will cover the entire width of the heart.

Cut the paper twist into the following strip lengths to make the red flag stripes:

Stripe No. 1 = 5 inches long
Stripes No. 3 and 5 = 8 inches long
Stripe No. 7 = 7 inches long
Stripe No. 9 = 10 inches long
Stripe No. 11 = 6 inches long
Stripe No. 13 = 3 inches long
Untwist and trim all of the paper twist strips to ¾ inch wide.

Paint all of the strips deep red and allow them to dry.

Beginning with Stripe No. 1 at the top of the heart, apply wood glue to the marked stripe area and fasten this strip in place, pleating or puckering it randomly for a wrinkled look. Alternating the colors of the red stripes with the white (pencil marked) stripes, repeat this process with the third, fifth, seventh, ninth, 11th and 13th stripes. The red stripes will hang over the edges. Allow them to dry, then tear off excess in a ragged pattern.

Paint the upper left quadrant of the heart dark blue. This area can be marked off by using the center fold and the bottom of the seventh stripe as a guide.

With white paint and a fine brush, paint the 13 stars in a circle in the center of the blue area using the pattern for star placement, *opposite.*

With a soft cloth, apply antique stain on both sides of the heart until the desired color is achieved. Spray the heart with the clear sealer. On the sample, we used a matte-finish sealer to achieve the antique look.

To hang the heart, punch holes with an ice pick 1 inch down from the center of each top lobe. Push ends of the jute through the holes from the back to the front and make an overhand knot approximately 1½ inches from each end. Fray the ends.

Americana Flag

Shown on page 19.

Finished flag is 16½x13 inches.

MATERIALS
Masking tape
6–8 standard-size brown paper grocery bags
16x20-inch sheet of heavy plastic, for a working surface
Wood glue
White, deep red, and dark blue acrylic paint
27-inch length of ¼-inch jute
Scissors; pencil
One 1-inch-wide and one fine-tip paintbrush
Tape measure
Antique stain
Clear acrylic spray sealer (matte-finish or gloss, depending on desired look)
Ice pick

INSTRUCTIONS
Note: The more ragged and wrinkled the flag appears while it is being formed, the better it will look when it is completed.

Use the masking tape to outline a 16½x13-inch rectangle on the heavy plastic work surface (a plastic cutting board or piece of acrylic plastic will work well).

This provides a guide for the formation of the flag. It is essential that you maintain a height of 13 inches, so the 1-inch stripes can be accurately measured. The width can vary slightly to achieve the desired ragged appearance.

Separate and cut away the sides and bottoms of 6 standard-size brown paper grocery bags. Use only the fronts and backs of the bags to make the flag.

Dampen the edges of the bag "backs" (the side with the seam) with water. Pinch out small portions of the paper bag around the edges to create a ragged effect.

After the edges are frayed, tear one sack lengthwise into strips approximately 2 inches wide. These tears should be uneven and irregular. Discard the center strip containing the seam and double thickness. Crumple the remaining strips until they appear wrinkled and worn.

Make a glue mixture of 2 parts glue and 1 part water. Dip each strip into the mixture, squeeze out excess liquid, then place the length of each strip horizontally on the plastic within the perimeters of the masking tape. Overlap each strip slightly, until the area within the taped rectangle is covered. The top and bottom edges should be parallel in order to measure and paint the stripes.

After the initial layer of strips from one sack "back" is formed into a rectangle, tear approximately 1 inch from the short top edge of 6 "front" portions of the sacks. Crumple each full "front" piece. Dip one piece into the glue mixture, and place it over the layers in the center of the rectangle formed of paper strips. Be sure all of the exposed paper edges are frayed and irregular.

Continue to apply a layer of the torn strips in this manner, and then alternate with a single "front" piece over the top of the strips. The finished size of the rectangle should be approximately 16½x13 inches.

continued

While the layered paper is still wet, slightly raise the center of the rectangle and curl the lower right edge for a furled effect. If necessary, carefully prop the raised and curled areas with household objects (such as a yard stick propped on edge, a rolling pin, or tin foil rolled to the desired size) that are covered with plastic wrap, so the areas will hold the shape you have placed them in. Allow the shaped paper rectangle to dry in this position.

When the shaped rectangle is dry, paint both sides with a white acrylic paint. Let dry. Measure and draw an 8-inch-wide and 7-inch-long rectangle in the upper left-hand corner. Paint this area dark blue.

Using a tape measure, measure and mark the right edge of the flag for thirteen 1-inch-wide stripes. Use the 1-inch brush to paint alternating stripes red. You will begin and end with red. The bottom of the 7th (red) stripe should come out even with the bottom of the blue rectangle.

Referring to the star placement guide on page 28, paint 13 white stars in a circle in the middle of the blue area. The shape of each star is similar to an asterisk symbol, only with 5 points.

If you wish, you can paint all the stripes on the back. All you need to do is paint the stripes on the edge that furls toward the front of the flag. See the photograph on page 19 for details.

Antique both sides of the flag to the desired color with antiquing stain, and spray with a clear sealer. For our sample, we used a matte-finish sealer to give the flag an antique appearance.

Punch holes with the ice pick in both upper corners of the flag 1½ inches from each edge. Push ends of the 27-inch length of ¼-inch jute through the flag from back to front. Tie overhand knots in the rope approximately 1½ inches from the ends. Fray the rope ends.

Anniversary Scherenschnitte

Shown on page 21.

Finished size of cut piece is 10x7½ inches.

MATERIALS

Good-quality 8½x11-inch bond paper
Tracing paper
Graphite paper, available at art and crafts stores
Newsprint paper pad
Mat board for mounting design
Sharp 4-inch embroidery or manicure scissors
Cosmetic silk sponge
Instant coffee for staining
White glue; stapler
Brown and black ink
Crow-quill pen

INSTRUCTIONS

Note: It is easier to cut scherenschnitte designs from papers that are thin and lightweight, such as parchment or bonded typing paper.

Trace the full-size pattern, *opposite*, onto tracing paper. Staple the reverse side of the traced pattern to the plain side of graphite paper. Position and staple the graphite paper over the scherenscnitte paper. The staples will keep your pattern from slipping.

With a sharp pencil, draw atop the tracing. Be careful to go over every line only once for proper registration. Remove the staples and separate the bond paper from the others.

Using the embroidery or manicure scissors, begin to cut the inside areas of the design first. Cut the outside area last. This technique allows for a larger area to grasp while cutting the tiny inside openings.

Always cut with the tips of the scissors, completely closing the tips at the end of each snip.

STAINING THE DESIGN: Prepare the staining solution by mixing 1 part instant coffee to 4 parts of water. Dip the silk sponge into the solution and lightly dab the stain on the paper cutting (the side without the graphite marks). Mix 3 more parts water to the coffee solution; dab the remaining areas, leaving more white spaces if you want a light stain and covering all the white areas for a darker stain.

Carefully lay the stained design between two to four sheets of plain newsprint, and place these layerings inside a telephone book. Weight down the telephone book with additional heavy books.

When the paper cutting is completely dry and crisp, inscribe the saying atop the design with a crow-quill pen. Use a blended mixture of slightly watered-down brown and black ink.

FRAMING THE DESIGN: Glass will hold the design flat, and tiny smears of white glue on the backs will hold the design to the mat board or the paper you choose. If you use raised mats around the cut paper, mount design completely with spray adhesive.

Rocking Horse Scherenschnitte

Shown on page 20.

Finished size of cut piece is 9½x7½ inches.

MATERIALS

Good-quality 8½x11-inch bond paper; tracing paper
Graphite paper, available at art and crafts stores
Newsprint paper pad
Mat board for mounting design
Sharp 4-inch embroidery scissors or manicure scissors
Cosmetic silk sponge
Instant coffee for staining
White glue; stapler
Brown and black ink
Crow-quill pen

INSTRUCTIONS

Trace the rocking horse pattern on page 32 onto tracing paper. Transfer the design to the paper. Cut and stain the paper following the instructions for the Anniversary Scherenschnitte, *left.*

ANNIVERSARY SCHERENSCHNITTE
Full-Size Pattern

ROCKING HORSE SCHERENSCHNITTE
Full-Size Pattern

FAVORITE TECHNIQUES

Papier-Mâché Duck Decoy and Fish Tray

Shown on pages 22 and 23.

Finished tray is 19½x11 inches.
Finished decoy is 17x8 inches.

MATERIALS
Aluminum wire
Needle-nose pliers
Wallpaper paste; newspaper
Acrylic paints in colors of your
    choice; watercolor brushes
White acrylic gesso
Spray varnish

INSTRUCTIONS

For the fish tray
BUILDING THE FRAME: Referring to the wire assemblage diagram, *top right*, twist wire to make an oval base approximately 8 inches long and 2 inches wide. Use needle-nose pliers to fasten the ends of the wire. Twist a second piece of wire to establish the fish shape, including the mouth and tail; fasten the ends. Add the wire fins to the shape by twisting one long wire around the base, up to the fish shape and extending beyond the fish shape. Make the three humps for the dorsal fin, twisting around the fish shape each time. Then referring to the side view diagram of the fish, *above right*, cut 3 equal lengths of wire and fasten each of these wires to both the sides of the base and the fish shape to establish the depth of the bowl.

COVERING THE SHAPE: In a medium-size container, mix the wallpaper paste with enough water to make a paste that is of gel-like consistency.

Tear or cut newspaper into 1½-inch-wide strips. Working with one strip at a time, dip the strip of paper in the paste and fasten the strip to the wire form. Cover the entire frame with three to four layers of newspaper strips. Allow some of the layers to dry before continuing to the next layer. Then turn the piece over and

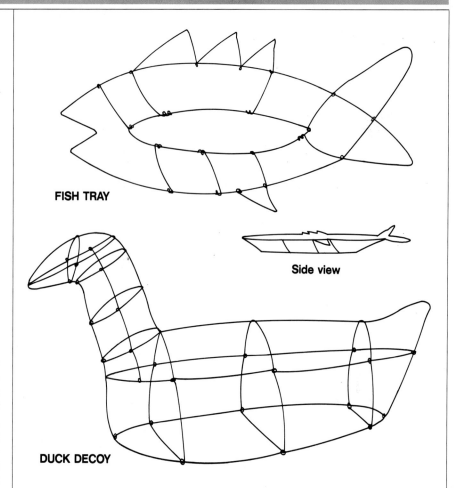

FISH TRAY

Side view

DUCK DECOY

paste the layers of paper on the underside of the frame. Let the piece dry completely.

PAINTING THE TRAY: Using the photograph on page 22 as a guide, draw defined areas for bold color areas on both the top and underside of the fish. Paint each of these areas with colors of your choice; let dry. Add additional painting embellishments in contrasting colors for interest. When dry, spray the piece with spray varnish.

For the duck decoy
BUILDING THE FRAME: Referring to the wire assemblage diagram *above*, twist wire to make a teardrop-shaped base approximately 10½ inches long and 5 inches wide. Use needle-nose pliers to fasten the ends of the wire. Make a second teardrop slightly larger than the base. Fasten these two shapes together with three wires to establish the body and hump of the back.

Run wires from the front end of the base to the second teardrop. Shape wire to establish the neck, head profile, and down and across the back, shaping the tail and fastening the wire at the back of the base. Build and strengthen the neck with three ovals.

Continue to build the neck and side of the face by running wires from both sides of the third oval of the neck to the front of the beak. Add a fourth oval around the head and beak area to define the eyes and side of the face.

Refer to the instructions for papier-mâchéing the fish tray in order to complete the shape of the decoy.

Using colors of your choice, paint large areas starting with the lower half of the duck, wing area, neck, head, and beak. Fill areas in with more detail such as dots and lines. See the photograph on page 23. Spray varnish over the completed decoy.

Papier-Mâché Tips and Techniques

Having fun with paper is not only fun, but it's also inexpensive. In addition to the projects that we've presented in this book (pages 18, 19, 22, and 23), here are some tips for working with this craft on your own and exploring some more of its possibilities.

To make your own batch of watered paste, bring a quart of water and ¼ cup of flour to a boil. Add more water, if necessary, so your mixture has the same consistency and appearance as milk. This paste should be used within a day or two and stored in the refrigerator when not being used.

An easy substitute for watered paste is white crafts glue or wallpaper paste. It must be watered down and used the same way as the flour and water paste.

When constructing three-dimensional objects, there are many items around the house to use for shapes and armatures. Tin cans, plastic bottles, boxes, cardboard tubes, egg cartons, chicken wire, balloons, old light bulbs, paper plates, and bowls can all serve as bases or parts for many papier-mâché objects.

You can use glass or ceramic bowls as forms to create shapes. Cover the outside of the bowl with plastic wrap or tin foil, and proceed to cover the bowl with pa-pier-mâché. Allow the paper to dry before removing the shape from the "bowl" mold.

There are several methods, depending on their uses, for making papier-mâché. When you tear newspaper, tissue paper, or paper towels into small pieces and soak them in the watered paste for at least 8 hours, you have a paper mixture that is well-suited to making finer objects such as pieces of jewelry.

If you want to create your own armatures from paper, use whole sheets of newspaper, and dip 3 or 4 sheets at a time into watered paste. Roll or bundle these sheets, and attach them to other rolls or bundles to begin the formation of the larger object. You also can fasten whole sheets of newspaper over large shapes, such as cardboard boxes or hand-built figures of chicken-wire frames.

Apply several coats of papier-mâché to your object, allowing each coat to dry. Paint the object with a white latex paint, and lightly sand any rough surfaces. Then paint the details, as desired, on the finished piece. When all the painting is complete, apply at least 2 coats of varnish to seal the surface and make the object water-resistant.

GLUING DESIGN: Mark center of tabletop with a 3-inch-wide "X" by drawing straight lines from corner to opposite corner. Begin gluing at the X. Brush glue across X and center a white square over the X. (Square is placed correctly if the drawn lines of the X appear at the corners of the square.) Following the manufacturer's instructions, decoupage the square in place.

Continue the decoupaging procedure, placing a brown square on each side of the white square. Glue the taupe squares around brown squares (see photograph on page 25).

To complete the center diamond, apply a row of black squares, then red, and end with white.

To fill the corners, add a row of medium-dark red squares along the white diamond edges. Then, working toward corners, follow with rows of brown, dark red, taupe, and white corner squares.

Decoupaged Tray

Shown on page 24.

Finished tray measures 15 inches in diameter.

MATERIALS
15-inch-diameter wooden tray
1 yard of dark red wall covering
1 yard of taupe wall covering
Taupe enamel; primer; brush
Fine sandpaper
Decoupage glue; ¾-inch-wide artist's brush
Straightedge
Pencil
Scissors or paper cutter

INSTRUCTIONS
Lightly sand, then paint the tray with primer; let dry. Lightly sand primed tray again for a smooth finish. Paint entire tray with taupe enamel. Let dry.

Cut twenty-one 2-inch squares from the red wallcovering. Cut twenty 2-inch squares from the taupe wall covering.

Wallpaper Tabletop

Shown on pages 24 and 25.

Finished size of tabletop is 22¾ inches square.

MATERIALS
10-inch-square pieces of paper wall covering in the following colors and amounts: one *each* of a black, red, medium-dark red, dark red, brown, and taupe print; two of a white print
22¾-inch-square white tabletop
Good-quality paper cutter
Decoupage glue; ¾-inch-wide artist's brush
Yardstick; pencil

INSTRUCTIONS
PREPARING SQUARES: Using a paper cutter and *exact* measurements, cut the wall covering into squares. (*Note:* When cutting the paper squares, even the most careful measuring will yield some slightly different sizes. Cut all of the paper to get enough squares from which to select the best ones.)

First, cut the 8 sheets of wall covering (2 at a time) into 2-inch-wide strips; then cut the strips into 2-inch squares. Sort and select 12 black, 16 red, 20 medium-dark red, 12 dark red, 25 white, 20 brown, and 16 taupe squares with the most exact 2-inch-square measurements.

Referring to the diagram *below,* locate and mark a guideline across the center of the tray with a pencil and straightedge. Draw another line perpendicular to this line in the center of the tray. Draw a guideline around the tray perimeter, marking off the border.

Place five red squares along the centerline as shown in the diagram. Following the instructions on the glue bottle, decoupage the first red square at the center of the tray. (*Note:* Square is placed correctly when the pencil guidelines appear at each corner of the square.) Use decoupage glue to fasten the next two squares on each side of the first square along the center guideline.

Before gluing the two squares at the border, place them in position and mark the border line on them. Cut away excess corner and decoupage the corner squares in place.

Working from the center outward, decoupage brown squares along the edges of the red squares checkerboard-style.

Continue this procedure until the tray center is covered. If desired, coat the tray with a second coat of decoupage glue or varnish.

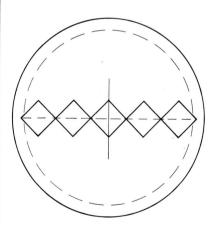

DECOUPAGED TRAY

Paper Wall Tile

Shown on page 24.

MATERIALS
For 1 square yard of wall area
Eight 2-inch squares of black adhesive-backed paper
Twenty-four 6-inch squares of white adhesive-backed paper
Metal yardstick; level; pencil
Off-white wall enamel
Brush or roller
Chalk line and plumb bob
Scissors or paper cutter

INSTRUCTIONS
PREPARATION: Fill any nail holes with surfacing compound, and lightly sand the rough areas of your wall. Paint the wall with off-white enamel.

Determine the amount of paper needed to cover the wall according to the materials list above. Cut the adhesive-backed paper into 2-inch black squares and 6-inch white squares by hand or with a paper cutter. For the white squares, refer to the diagram *above right.* Measure and mark a point 1½ inches on each side of one corner only; connect the two points with a diagonal pencil line. Cut away that corner. Cut the corner on each of the white squares.

Use a chalk line and plumb bob to mark a vertical line in the center of your wall.

HANGING THE TILE: Remove the backing from the first white square and place it at the top or bottom of the wall along the plumb line. (The cutaway tip can be placed at the top or bottom of the line). Place the second white tile along the plumb line, leaving ⅛-inch gap (grout line) and positioning the cutaway tip correctly as shown in the diagram at *right.* It takes four white squares to complete one pattern repeat. Continue working along the plumb line until the top or bottom of the wall is reached.

With the level, mark a horizontal line across the top of one tile near the center of the wall. This will give you a visual check for keeping the tiles in line as you work. Work another vertical row of tiles along the first row of tiles following the diagram and creating empty diamond-shaped gaps for the placement of the black squares. Fill the empty diamonds with a black square.

Continue working up, down, and across the wall to complete the surface.

Note: Mark new plumb and level lines as you place tiles to keep the work straight. Don't worry if the "grout" lines between the tiles vary slightly. They will blend in the overall look.

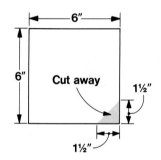

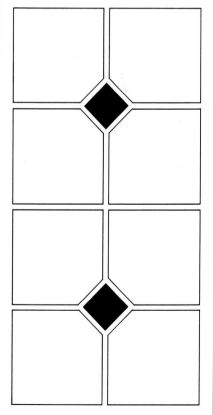

PAPER WALL TILE

A BIRTHDAY PARTY

UNDER THE BIG TENT

The sights, the sounds, the magic! Children are captivated by the circus and all it has to offer. So, what could be better inspiration for a special birthday party than colorful circus attractions? Step right up and see— here and on the following pages— the sensational selection of paper crafts projects you can make for your own three-ring celebration.

Star performers at this birthday party under the big tent include child-pleasing party favors, games, and decorations. Parents will be pleased as punch to find all the materials required for these projects are inexpensive and readily available.

In the center ring of our birthday celebration is a party table set with familiar circus sights. It's easy to see why this birthday cake belongs in the spotlight. Decorated with candy and animal cookies, the cake is placed on an empty ice-cream drum that's covered with wrapping paper and metallic poster board. A carousel top, also crafted from poster board, rests atop the candy sticks.

Fashion whimsical clown and animal wagon place mats from poster board to protect the party table. When the party's over, they make charming wall decorations for a child's bedroom.

The coordinating napkin rings are actually 2-inch pieces of empty wrapping-paper tubes patterned to look like miniature circus drums.

Instructions for all the projects in this fun-filled chapter begin on page 46.

It's a party, so put on a happy face. The grinning clown's face *opposite* consists of a big poster board smile and a confetti-dotted papier-mâché nose.

Other festive party favors include the dress-up ties and jumping jacks *opposite*. For more about these projects, see page 45.

The circus mobile *above* is bound to bring back birthday memories long after the guests have gone home. Make this delightful party decoration with an ice-cream drum, poster board in various colors, and assorted round stickers. Use fishing line to hang the circus figures.

A BIRTHDAY PARTY

There's no doubt about it—kids get a kick out of clowning around. When you introduce this bright clown photo board into the party's festivities, the kids will line up lickety-split. Parents can get a glimpse of the party's fun if you use an instant camera and send pictures home with each child.

To make a photo board, use a piece of foam-core board for the background and carefully cut out the hand and head openings. For the decorating pieces, choose colorful papers of all kinds—poster board, wallpaper, and wrapping and construction paper, or whatever else you have on hand. Embellish the board with imaginative odds and ends, such as disposable plastic plates, pom-poms, balloons, stickers, and a fancy bow tie.

Depending on the average height of the children attending the party, you may want to adjust the height of the board so each child may kneel comfortably while his or her photo is taken. To increase the height, add a wrapping paper road for the car to "drive" on.

From toddlers to teens, few children can resist a few swift swings at a piñata. And no matter who strikes the final blow, everyone wins as the sweet treats tumble to the floor. Is it any wonder this spirited activity remains a party favorite?

The colorful piñatas *above* and *opposite* are easy to construct from papier-mâché. Use balloons to form the heads and bodies. Cardboard tubes of various lengths work nicely for arms, necks, and legs.

Decorate the piñata as desired. Our circus creatures sport a fanciful finish produced by overlapping pieces of torn tissue paper. You also could paint your creature in wild colors to give it a personality all its own.

Imagination is the key to making animal piñatas of all kinds. Take a creative look at everyday throwaways, and you're sure to find all the materials you need. Egg cartons, for example, can be used for a lion's mane or the spikes down a dinosaur's back. Or, you can fashion elephant ears from a pair of paper plates.

A BIRTHDAY PARTY

The best birthday parties include a fast-paced game or two. And kids of all ages will surely enjoy a rollicking game of "toss the beanbag."

To craft this clown game, *opposite*, cut openings from a piece of foam-core board. Then, glue the clown's face in place using poster board pieces.

Bright pieces of poster board and other colorful paper products make up the playful jumping jacks and the oversize ties *above*. Make one for each party guest before the party begins. Or, plan the ties as a party activity, and let the children decorate their own ties with assorted stickers and colored tapes or crayons.

CIRCUS CAGE PLACE MAT
Full-Size Pattern

Green wheels Cut 2
Black Cut 1 with wheels
Silver Cut 1 without wheels
Fold
Wheel
Placement

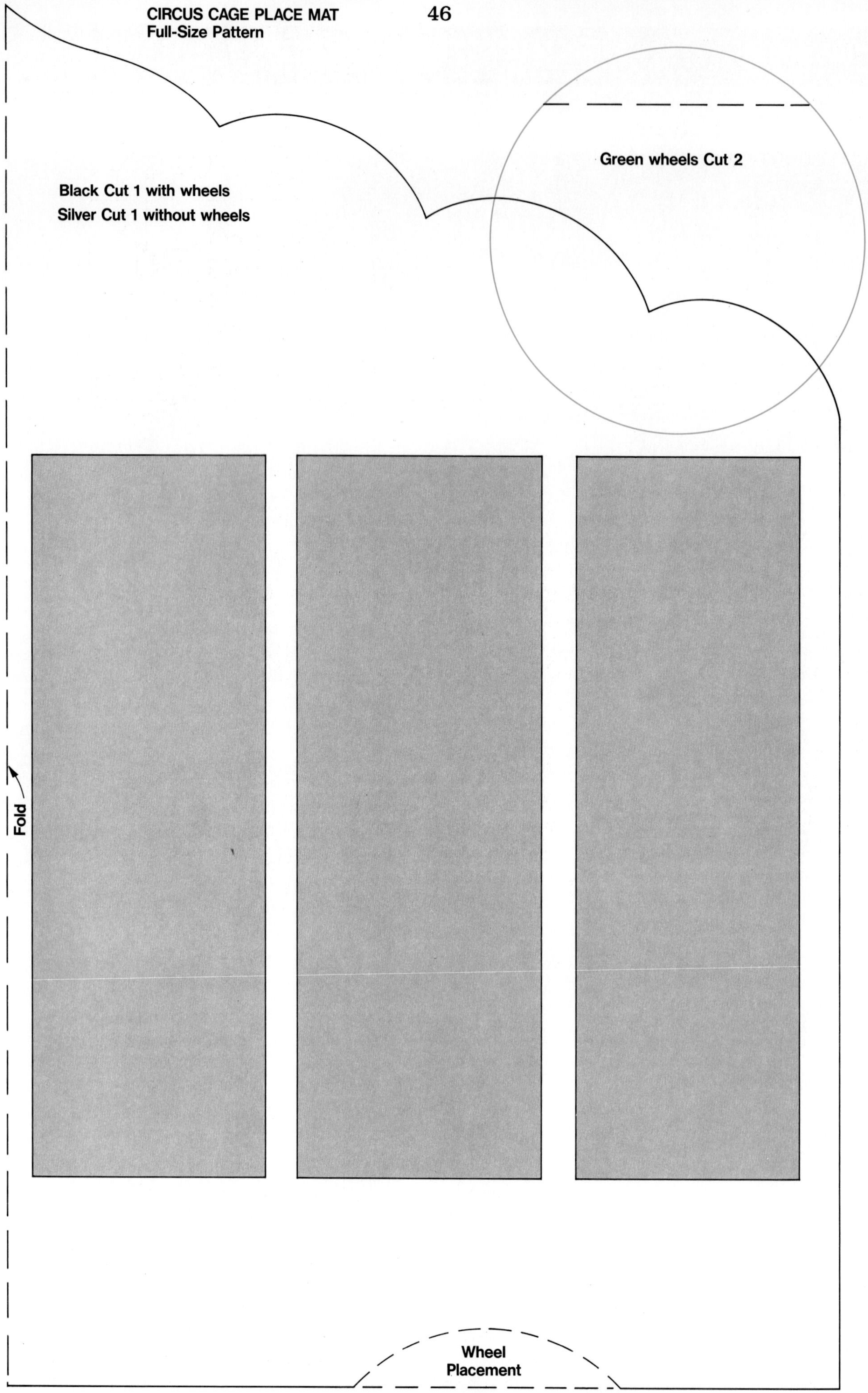

Circus Place Mats And Napkin Rings

Shown on pages 36 and 37.

Finished clown place mat is 16½x15½ inches. Finished cage place mats are 13¾x13½ inches.

MATERIALS
Poster board in assorted colors of your choice plus black and silver metallic poster board
Colored tapes; assorted stickers
Crafts glue; scissors
Pipe cleaner for flower stem
Felt markers; confetti dots
Construction paper for the napkin rings
Empty wrapping-paper tubes

INSTRUCTIONS
For the clown place mat
Enlarge the clown pattern, *bottom right*. Cut one clown head shape from yellow poster board, excluding the flower and stem.

Referring to photo on page 36, cut shapes from assorted colors of poster board to make the face details. Glue shapes to the yellow head piece.

Cut two flower shapes; glue them together over one end of the pipe cleaner. Cut two leaves and glue over the pipe cleaner; glue end of pipe cleaner to back of hat.

For the cage place mat
Using the full-size pattern *opposite* cut one cage from black poster board. Cut one silver cage, removing the shaded areas.

Cut giraffes and lions from poster board using patterns on pages 52 and 54. Trim giraffes with stickers and lions with orange and yellow poster board. Referring to the diagrams at *right*, glue silver cage atop black cage, gluing animals in place at the same time.

Cut two wheels; glue wheels to cage using the placement markings on the pattern as a guide.

Decorate mats using stickers and markers, as desired.

continued

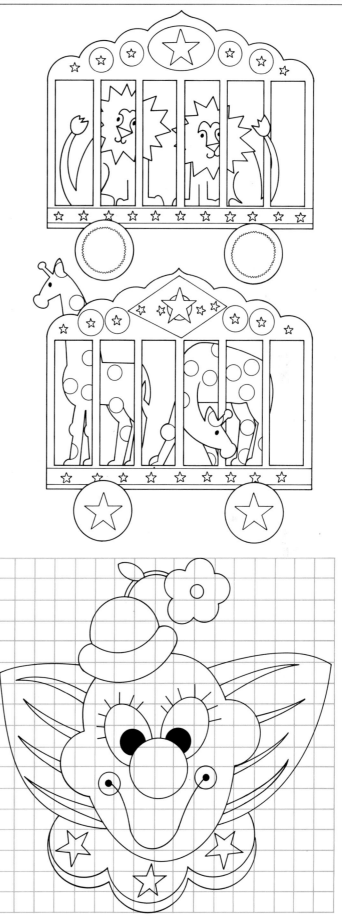

CIRCUS PLACE MATS　　　　　**1 Square = 1 Inch**

For the napkin rings

Mark off and cut 2-inch-long pieces from the wrapping-paper tubes. Cover the pieces with construction paper. Cut ⅜-inch-wide strips of metallic poster board, and glue the strips around the top and bottom edges of each tube.

Glue confetti dots evenly spaced around the edges of one outside strip. Glue dots on the other outside strip halfway between the dots on the first strip.

Use a marker to draw a zigzag line around the tube connecting the dots from one band to the other band.

Carousel Cake And Drum Base

Shown on page 36.

Drum is 9½ inches in diameter.

MATERIALS

1 empty, round 3-gallon ice-cream drum
Scissors; hot-glue gun
Decorative round stickers, stars, and tapes; wrapping paper
Gold metallic poster board
Scrap of blue poster board for the flag; crafts glue
Gift-wrapping cord

For the cake

One 8-inch double layer cake
Frosting; candy gumdrops
Six 6-inch-long candy sticks
6 decorated animal cookies
1 toothpick

INSTRUCTIONS
For the drum base

Measure and mark a line 7 inches up from the bottom of the ice-cream drum. Cut along line.

Cut an 8-inch-long piece of wrapping paper to fit around the drum plus a ½-inch overlap. Glue paper to the outside of the drum, overlapping the edges and gluing the extra 1 inch to the inside of the drum at the top.

Cut two 1½-inch-wide strips of gold metallic poster board, ½ inch longer than the drum circumference. Glue strips along bottom and top edges of drum.

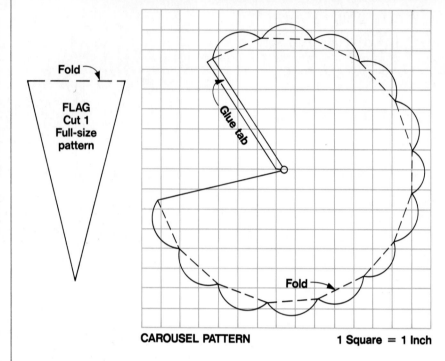

Fold →

FLAG
Cut 1
Full-size
pattern

Glue tab

Fold →

CAROUSEL PATTERN   1 Square = 1 Inch

Decorate the top and bottom strips with round stickers. Fasten stickers on the bottom band halfway between the stickers on the top band. Referring to the photo on page 36, zigzag the cording between the stickers on the two bands, spot gluing the cord along the edges of the bands.

Place a plastic plate on top of the drum to hold the cake.

For the cake

Place the cake on the plate. Frost the cake and position the candy sticks vertically at equal intervals along the sides of the cake. Place one decorated animal cookie between *each* candy stick. Dip gumdrop bases in frosting and decorate sides of cake as desired.

Enlarge the carousel pattern *above*. Cut carousel from gold poster board. Fold the scallops down along the fold lines. Glue the tab to the underside of the other edge. Refer to the photo on page 36 to trim the carousel top.

Cut one flag from blue poster board using the pattern *above*. Fold flag in half and glue toothpick to inside along the fold. Insert toothpick into gumdrop. Glue gumdrop to top of the carousel. Rest the carousel on top of the candy sticks.

Giraffe and Lion Piñatas

Shown on pages 42 and 43.

The giraffe is 25 inches tall; the lion is 17 inches tall.

MATERIALS

Old newspapers
Empty cardboard tubes
Egg cartons for lion's mane
Balloons
Flour; water
Gesso
Masking tape; hot-glue gun
Scissors
Waxed paper
Flat white spray paint
String; movable eyes
Colored tissue paper or paint

INSTRUCTIONS

For either animal, use balloons for the heads and bodies and empty gift-wrap tubes for necks, arms and legs. Do not hesitate to be creative with the creature's shape.

Tear newspapers into 1x6-inch strips.

Mix flour and water together until it is the consistency of thick cream. Paste might thicken as it stands; add water to thin.

Keeping all body parts separate, begin covering the balloons with overlapping strips of newspaper dipped in paste. Continue layering paper for at least 2 layers, alternating the direction and overlapping strips for better coverage. You should not be able to see any of the color from the balloon through the paper layers.

Set pieces aside on waxed paper to dry for about 2 days. Check shapes and turn as they dry, or a flattened spot might occur.

After shapes are dry, hot-glue your animal body, including the tube legs, together. If you are making the lion, glue the cut segments of the egg cartons to the head. For ease in working, tie a 45-inch-long string or ribbon around the main part of the body. This will enable you to hang the piñata to work on it.

Add more newspaper strips to cover the joints, string, or weak spots. The tubes do not need to be covered if they are made from firm cardboard. Let dry while hanging.

Spray-paint entire animal with flat white paint. Let dry.

The piñata can be decorated in several ways. Use acrylic paint in wild colors to personalize your piñata. Or tear colored tissue paper into odd shapes, and use the gesso to glue the paper to the animal as shown in our samples on pages 42 and 43. Overlap the tissue paper shapes, and "paint" the gesso over the colored tissue paper. The pattern will develop as overlapping occurs. Cover the entire animal with the colored tissue paper.

To get a fringed look for the lion's mane, cut several rows of colored tissue paper 2 inches wide and the length of the paper. To fringe the paper, begin at one end and cut 1½-inch-long slashes every ¼ inch along the entire length of the paper. Run a bead of glue along the uncut edge of the strip, and fasten around the face.

When the piñata is completely covered with paint or paper, glue on the eyes. Make a yarn tail, and glue it to the body.

To add ears, cut slits in the top of the head, and glue in small triangular pieces of decorated cardboard. Tie ribbons to the tail and around the neck.

Cut out a 1-inch-square piece from the back of the animal, being careful not to drop the piece inside. Save the piece you remove.

Fill the animal with small pieces of wrapped candy, gum, and small toys.

Use the hot-glue gun to re-fasten the 1-inch-square piece. Use the gesso to glue a few strips of tissue paper over the repaired hole.

Hang the piñata, and have the children take turns trying to break it open.

Dress-Up Ties

Shown on pages 38 and 45.

The ties range from 7¾x15½ inches to 12½x5¼ inches.

MATERIALS
Assorted colors of poster board
Large safety pins
Clear tape
Assorted stickers and colored tapes
Graph paper
Scissors

INSTRUCTIONS
Refer to the tie patterns on page 50. Enlarge the patterns of your choice onto graph paper. For the necktie, align the A-B lines on the pattern to make one pattern.

Cut the shapes from assorted colors of poster board. Create your own tie shapes using some of the ideas shown in the photographs on pages 38 and 45.

Decorate the ties with stickers, tapes, or crayons. Or use the ties as a party activity, and let the children trim their own ties.

Tape a large safety pin to the back of the tie knots so you can pin them to the children's clothes.

Papier-Mâché Nose and Mouth

Shown on page 38.

MATERIALS
Newspapers
Balloons
Flour
Water
Acrylic paint
Paintbrush
Heavy elastic thread
Red or orange poster board
Sequins or confetti dots
Black marker
Scissors
White crafts glue
Hot-glue gun

INSTRUCTIONS
Tear the newspaper into strips approximately ½x2 inches.

Blow up a balloon until it is the size you would like for a nose.

Mix flour and water together until it is the consistency of thick cream. The paste might thicken as it stands; add water to thin.

Dip strips into the paste, and cover three-quarters of the balloon with the pasted strips. Apply at least two coverings of the strips, overlapping them as you work. Set the balloon on a piece of waxed paper to dry for two days.

Break the balloon, and carefully remove it from the papier-mâché. Check for weak spots, and add more paste strips if necessary. Trim the edge smooth with scissors for the nose opening.

Paint the nose as desired.

Enlarge the mouth pattern on page 50 onto graph paper. Cut mouth from orange poster board, and glue it to the bottom of the nose with the hot-glue gun. Use a black marker to draw the center line of the mouth.

Use crafts glue to decorate the nose with sequins, or trim with confetti dots.

Punch two holes in each side of the nose. Cut elastic the size of the child's head. Insert the ends into the two holes, and knot the ends. Slip nose and mouth over child's head as you would a mask.

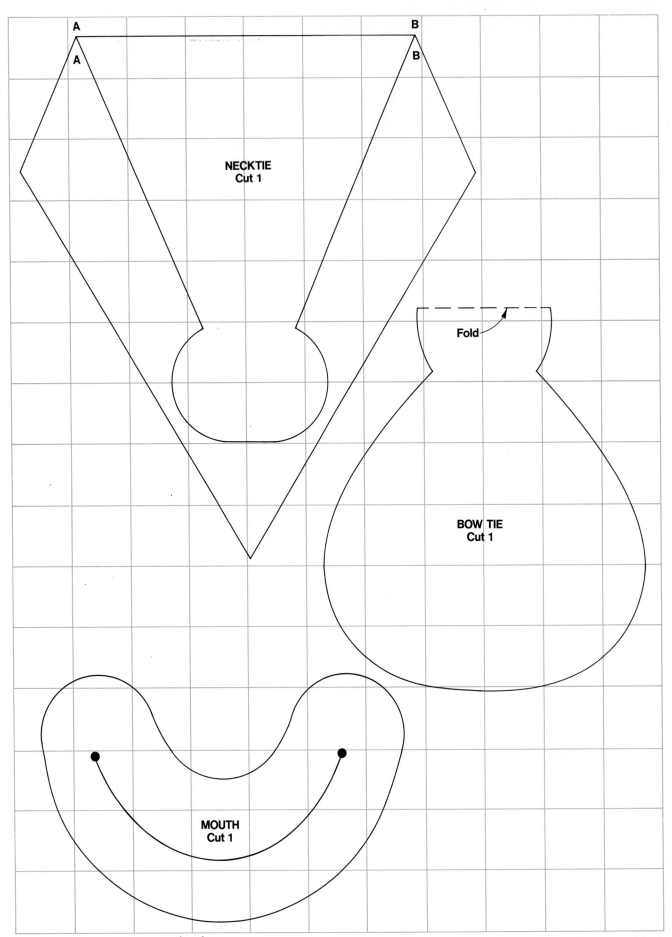

NECKTIE
Cut 1

A

A

B

B

Fold

BOW TIE
Cut 1

MOUTH
Cut 1

DRESS-UP TIES AND PAPIER-MÂCHÉ NOSE AND MOUTH

1 Square = 1 Inch

A BIRTHDAY PARTY

Circus Mobile

Shown on page 39.

MATERIALS
Poster board in various colors and silver metallic poster board
Scraps of wrapping paper
Round stickers in assorted sizes
One 3-gallon ice-cream drum
Permanent markers
Rub-off letters
Crafts glue or hot-glue gun
Scissors
Transparent nylon thread or fishing line

INSTRUCTIONS
To make the ring, measure 2 inches down from the metal rim on the open end of the ice-cream drum. Cut carefully along this line. Cut two 2-inch strips of silver metallic poster board ½ inch longer than the circumference of the ring. Glue one silver strip to the outside of the ring and the other silver strip on the inside of the ring. Overlap the excess of each strip. Decorate the outside of the ring with large round, colored stickers.

Punch three small holes evenly spaced around the top (the edge with the metal rim) of the ring. Punch five holes evenly spaced around the bottom of the ring.

Trace the pattern shapes at *right* and those on pages 52, 53, and 54. Transfer shapes to the poster board in colors of your choice. Cut out shapes and decorate as desired with markers, stickers, and letters.

The popcorn box was decorated with a scrap of dotted wrapping paper.

The cage has four green wheels, which are glued in the same two places on both sides of the cage.

Refer to the photograph on page 39 for decorating ideas. All hanging figures are decorated on both sides.

To make the hanger, cut three 2-yard lengths of nylon thread, and insert one through each of the three top holes on the ring, drawing all ends up evenly. Holding all of the threads together as one tie a knot approximately 10 inches up from the ring.

To hang the mobile figures, carefully make a small hole in the top of each figure. Thread an 18-inch length of nylon thread through each hole and tie.

Tie the nylon thread belonging to each of the figures to a bottom hole. Vary the length of each thread; tie a knot, and cut the remaining thread.

Secure all knots with a drop of crafts glue.

Hang the mobile in a doorway, or from the ceiling or a tree.

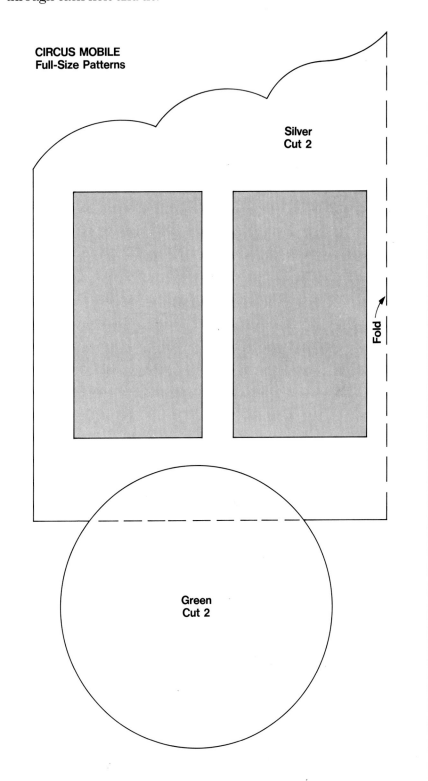

**CIRCUS MOBILE
Full-Size Patterns**

Silver
Cut 2

Fold

Green
Cut 2

CAGE MAT GIRAFFE

CIRCUS MOBILE GIRAFFE

POPCORN

**CAGE MAT AND
CIRCUS MOBILE
Full-Size Patterns**

A BIRTHDAY PARTY

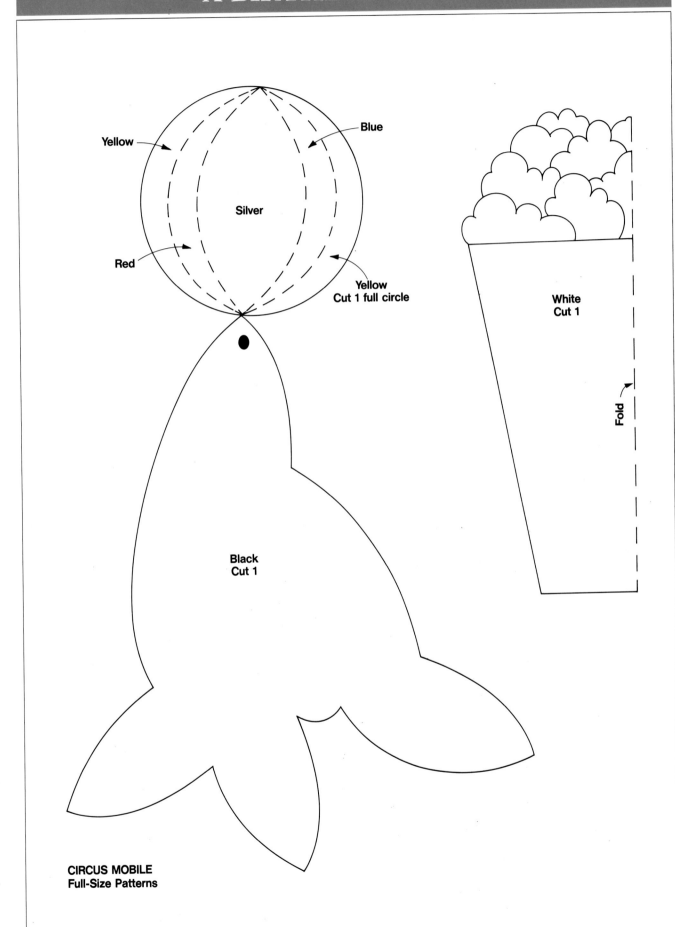

Yellow

Blue

Silver

Red

Yellow
Cut 1 full circle

White
Cut 1

Fold

Black
Cut 1

CIRCUS MOBILE
Full-Size Patterns

CAGE MAT
GIRAFFE
Full-Size Pattern

Yellow
Cut 2
for mobile

Orange
Cut 2
for mobile

Orange
Cut 2
for mobile

Yellow
Cut 1

CIRCUS MOBILE AND
CAGE MAT LION
Full-Size Patterns

A BIRTHDAY PARTY

Jumping Jack Party Favors

Shown on pages 38 and 45.
Party favors range from 12 to 13 inches, without stick.

MATERIALS
Poster board in assorted colors
Stickers and colored tapes
1/8-inch-diameter wooden dowels
 cut into 13-inch lengths
Scissors; hot-glue gun
Paper brads
Permanent ink marking pens
Curling ribbon for hair
Small-hole paper punch or awl

INSTRUCTIONS
Full-size patterns for the jumping jacks are at *right* and on page 56. The cutting directions on the patterns will make one jumping jack. *Note:* There are three body and two head patterns on page 56 to choose from. See the photo on page 45 to select the jumping jack you wish to make.

Trace, then transfer the patterns to assorted colors of poster board; cut out the shapes.

Use hot glue to attach hands to backs of lower arms and feet to backs of lower legs.

Use the paper punch to punch holes on arm and leg pieces as indicated by dots on patterns. Match holes for upper and lower parts of legs and arms, and insert brads to hold pieces together.

Glue each head to each body along the chin, making sure the two head and body pieces match.

Using pens and stickers, decorate all pieces as desired, establishing a front and a back side of the jumping jack.

Glue 3 inches of the dowel to wrong side (inside) of back.

Curl ribbon for hair, and glue to the wrong side (inside) of the head back. Glue heads together. Do not glue the bodies together.

Holding both body pieces together, punch holes at dot markings on the patterns.

Insert arms and legs *between* the two body pieces; insert brads through all layers to fasten to body. Keep the brads loose so the toy will dance when twirled.

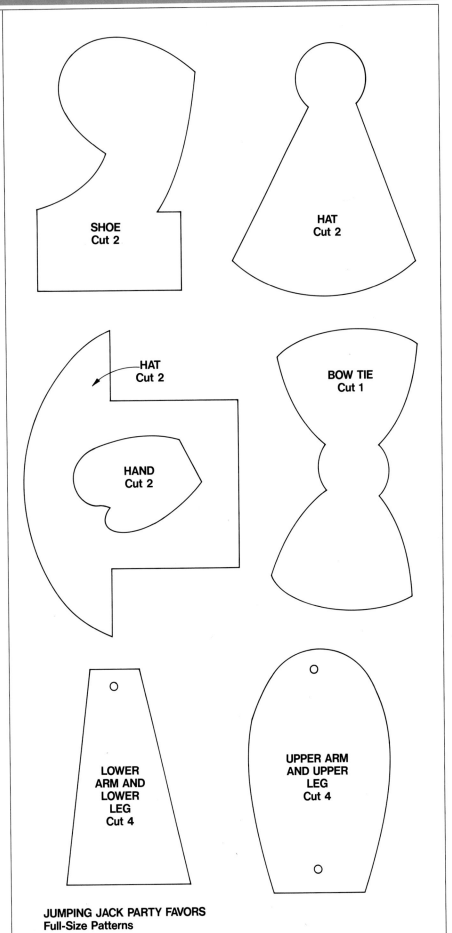

SHOE
Cut 2

HAT
Cut 2

HAT
Cut 2

HAND
Cut 2

BOW TIE
Cut 1

LOWER
ARM AND
LOWER
LEG
Cut 4

UPPER ARM
AND UPPER
LEG
Cut 4

JUMPING JACK PARTY FAVORS
Full-Size Patterns

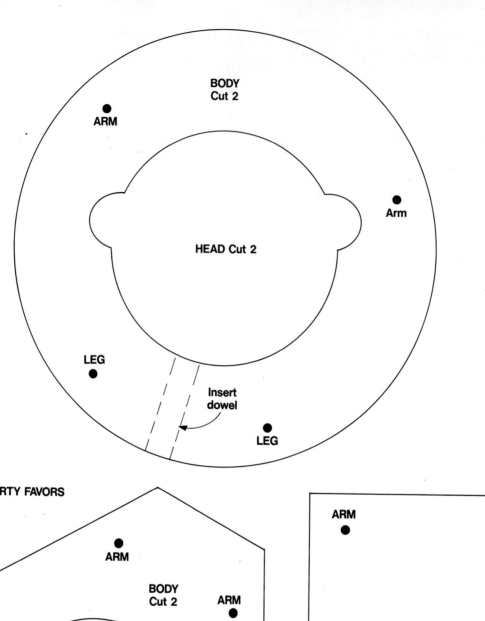

BODY
Cut 2

ARM

Arm

HEAD Cut 2

LEG

Insert
dowel

LEG

JUMPING JACK PARTY FAVORS
Full-Size Patterns

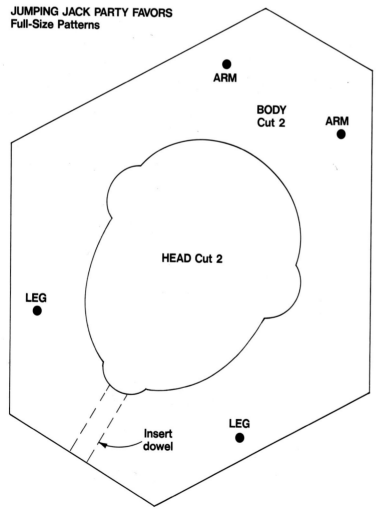

ARM

BODY
Cut 2

ARM

HEAD Cut 2

LEG

LEG

Insert
dowel

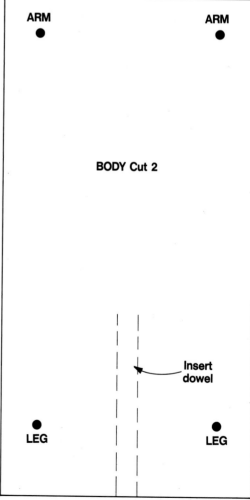

ARM

ARM

BODY Cut 2

Insert
dowel

LEG

LEG

A BIRTHDAY PARTY

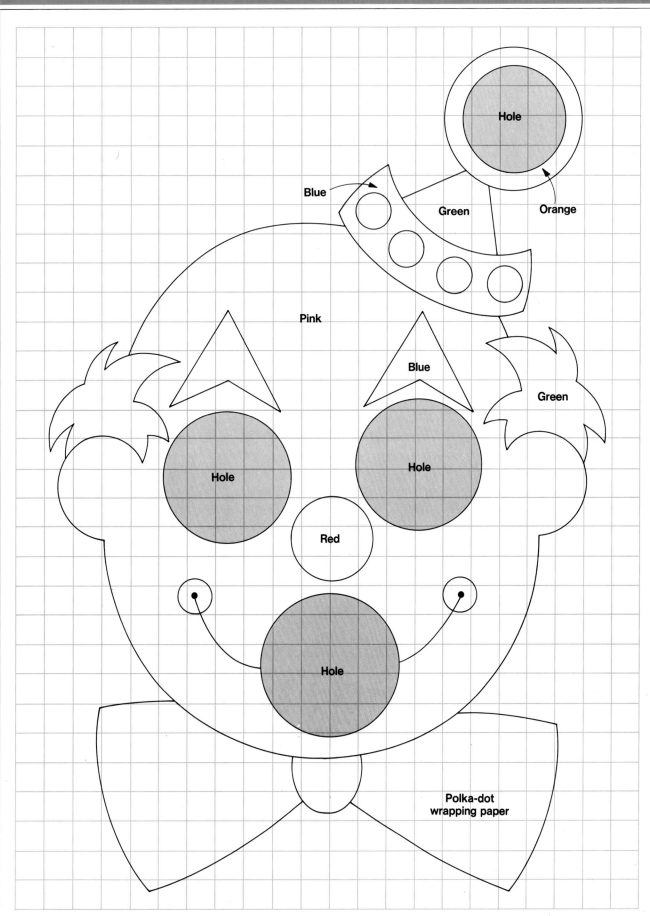

CLOWN PARTY GAME BOARD

1 Square = 1 Inch

Clown Party Game Board

Shown on page 44.

Finished board game measures 24x30 inches.

MATERIALS
24x30-inch piece of foam-core board
Assorted colors of poster board and wrapping paper scraps
Crafts knife
Sandpaper
Permanent markers
Assorted stickers and tapes
Crafts glue
Scissors

For the beanbags
Scraps of cotton fabric
Bag of dried beans (small beans, such as lentils)
Thread

INSTRUCTIONS
Enlarge the pattern on page 57 onto a large sheet of paper. Transfer pattern to foam-core board.

Using the crafts knife, carefully cut out the areas that are shaded on the pattern from the board. Use sandpaper to sand smooth the cut edges.

Use the original pattern to make separate patterns for the face, hair, nose, eyelashes, hat parts, and bow tie. Cut out these pattern shapes.

Trace around these pattern shapes onto the assorted colors of poster board, using colors of your choice or following the colors noted on the pattern on page 57.

Beginning with the clown's face, glue the pieces to the board. Carefully position pieces around holes. If necessary, use the crafts knife to trim the face poster board piece to fit around the holes of the board.

After all pieces are glued in place, decorate the clown with stickers, markers, tapes, and wrapping paper as shown in the photo on page 44.

Our bow tie is made from wrapping paper but could be made from poster board with round or star stickers added.

Make three flat, 2-inch-square beanbags, or use wads of paper to toss at the openings in the board.

BEANBAGS: To make one 2-inch beanbag cut two 3-inch-squares of cotton fabric. With right sides together, sew along three sides using ½-inch seam allowance. Turn bag right side out. Fill partially with dry beans. Slip-stitch the opening closed.

RULES OF THE GAME: Establish point values for each of the openings on the board. For example, the hole at the top of the board could be worth 30 points; the eye openings, 10 points each; and the mouth opening, 25 points.

For each turn, each child throws three bags. After each child has three turns, tally the points. The child with the highest number of points wins the game.

Happy Clown Photo Board

Shown on pages 40 and 41.

Finished photo board measures 40x45 inches.

MATERIALS
Poster board in various colors
Wrapping paper scraps
40x60-inch piece of foam-core board
Stick-on letter set (optional)
One 8½x11-inch sheet of construction paper, for the horn
1 balloon; 1 pom-pom
1 purchased bow tie
Two 9-inch luncheon-sized plastic plates for the wheels
Crafts glue; crafts knife
Scissors; sandpaper
Assorted stickers and tapes
Permanent markers

INSTRUCTIONS
Use the crafts knife to cut the top 15 inches from the foam-core board so that the piece measures 40x45 inches.

Enlarge the pattern opposite onto a large sheet of paper; note the shaded areas for the head and the hand holding the umbrella. Transfer the pattern to the board.

Carefully cut out the head and hand areas using the crafts knife. Be sure to leave the handle section of the umbrella in place. (The children hold onto the umbrella handle when they are having their picture taken.) Smooth the cut areas with sandpaper.

Use the original pattern to make separate patterns for all the details on the board. Trace and cut all pieces from assorted colors of poster board or wrapping paper. We used wrapping paper for the clown's shirt and the road. Refer to photograph on page 41.

Cut the horn shape from construction paper. Locate the center of the straight edge, and from this point bend both halves of the straight edge around to meet each other to form a cone shape; glue the straight edges together.

Begin gluing the poster board parts onto the foam-core board, beginning with the clown shirt and car. Glue all other pieces in place, noting that sometimes the pieces overlap. For example, when assembling the umbrella on the board, first glue the handle, then the covering, and finally the top.

Poke a hole in the foam-core board approximately ¾ inch behind the horn. Insert a blown-up balloon, from the back to the front, through the opening.

Use a dark permanent marker to draw around the shapes so they stand out better. A broad-tip marker works best.

Glue the plastic-plate wheels onto the car. Attach a pom-pom at the top of the clown's hat. Add a fun bow tie just below the head opening.

Finish the photo board by decorating it with stickers, stars, colored tapes, markers, and wrapping papers. Use the stick-on letters to spell out the word "circus" on the sign or use a black marker to write the letters.

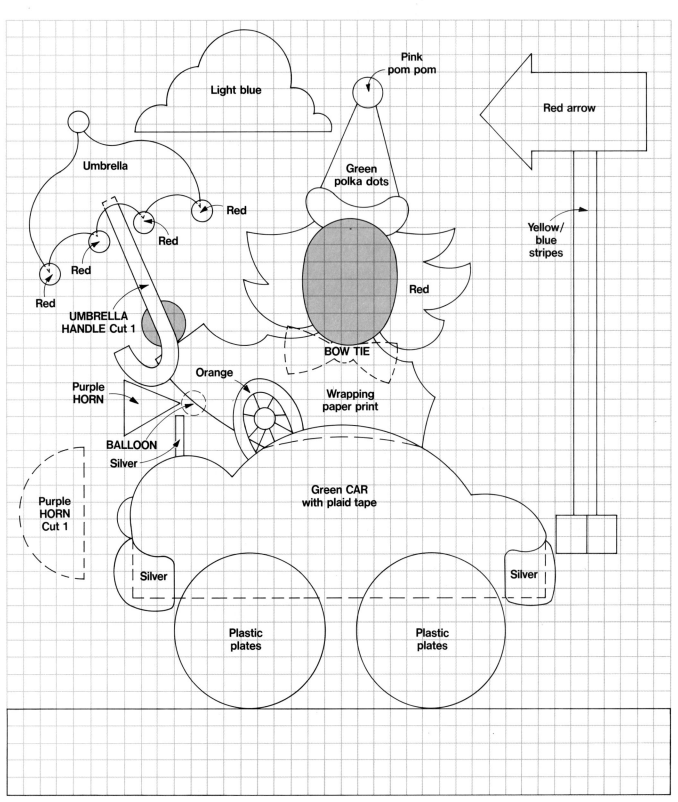

Light blue

Pink
pom pom

Red arrow

Umbrella

Green
polka dots

Red

Red

Yellow/
blue
stripes

Red

Red

Red

Red

UMBRELLA
HANDLE Cut 1

BOW TIE

Orange

Purple
HORN

Wrapping
paper print

BALLOON

Silver

Green CAR
with plaid tape

Purple
HORN
Cut 1

Silver

Silver

Plastic
plates

Plastic
plates

CLOWN PHOTO BOARD

1 Square = 1 Inch

PAPER MERRIMENT

FOR CHRISTMAS

At Christmastime, the versatility of working with paper becomes especially apparent. Festive centerpieces, greeting cards, ornaments and other decorations are among the many imaginative things you can make using various paper-craft techniques. Take a peek at the projects pictured here and on the following pages for great ideas for holiday decorations that can be made in a twinkling.

Perhaps the most captivating of all Christmas poems, Clement C. Moore's "The Night Before Christmas" has inspired countless crafters over the years. This year, create the spirit of this story in your home by making the enchanting centerpiece shown at *left*.

The materials required for this child-pleasing decoration are inexpensive and readily available. Santa's sleigh is actually a wine bottle basket filled with greenery and gaily wrapped packages. We added the chipboard to complete his vehicle.

Santa is crafted from crepe paper, plastic-foam balls, and other odds and ends. (For more about the Santa figure, please see page 63.)

The three reindeer are easily fashioned from chipboard and covered with torn pieces of rice paper. Add bows and bells for the finishing touches.

This reindeer design lends itself for use in other crafts. For example, use the pattern to make fabric or felt appliqués to decorate tree skirts, tablecloths, place mats, and sweatshirts.

PAPER MERRIMENT

The familiar figure of jolly old St. Nick is a merry addition to any holiday home. Crepe paper, glued to foam balls and trimmed with cotton batting, magically captures the spirit of Santa. A touch of paint or crayon adds the blush to his cheek and puts a twinkle in his eye.

The Santa *opposite* stands 12 inches tall, and the roly-poly ornament *above* is 5½ inches high.

Both projects use the same basic techniques. So, once you master the method, you can make lots of these little Santas. The ornament is the perfect size for a package topper, and this Santa is also the driver of the sleigh and reindeer centerpiece shown on page 60.

Herald the season's message with this personalized pop-up angel card, *above.*

The trumpeting greeting card is made from just two pieces of paper. The front of the 5x4-inch card features the musical score of a favorite Christmas carol.

Colored pencils add shading to the angel inside, which is easily traced, marked, and cut from a single piece of parchment.

A festive tree is the center of the home during the holidays. So let a grouping of

miniature trees like the ones at *right* be your symbol of giving and sharing. The three sizes (6¼, 8, and 10 inches high) make a pretty centerpiece. Cut them on the fold like traditional

paper dolls. Then unfold the cut trees, hand-sew three of them together along the center fold, and you've created a great three-dimensional decoration.

PAPER MERRIMENT

Express your best wishes for the Christmas season by making one-of-a-kind cards and gift tags. The cross-stitch designs at *left* are worked with embroidery floss on perforated paper. Once stitched, the embroidered pieces are trimmed and glued to colored card-stock paper.

To further the use of these holiday motifs, make miniature Christmas samplers with either of the card designs by substituting even-weave fabric for the paper. Or, use portions of the card and gift tag designs to make tree ornaments.

With one sheet of paper and a pair of scissors, you can craft a wall plaque as pretty as those *below*.

Precise folding and careful cutting are the keys to success when creating such intricate snowflake patterns as these. Try your hand at creating your own designs using our step-by-step folding instructions.

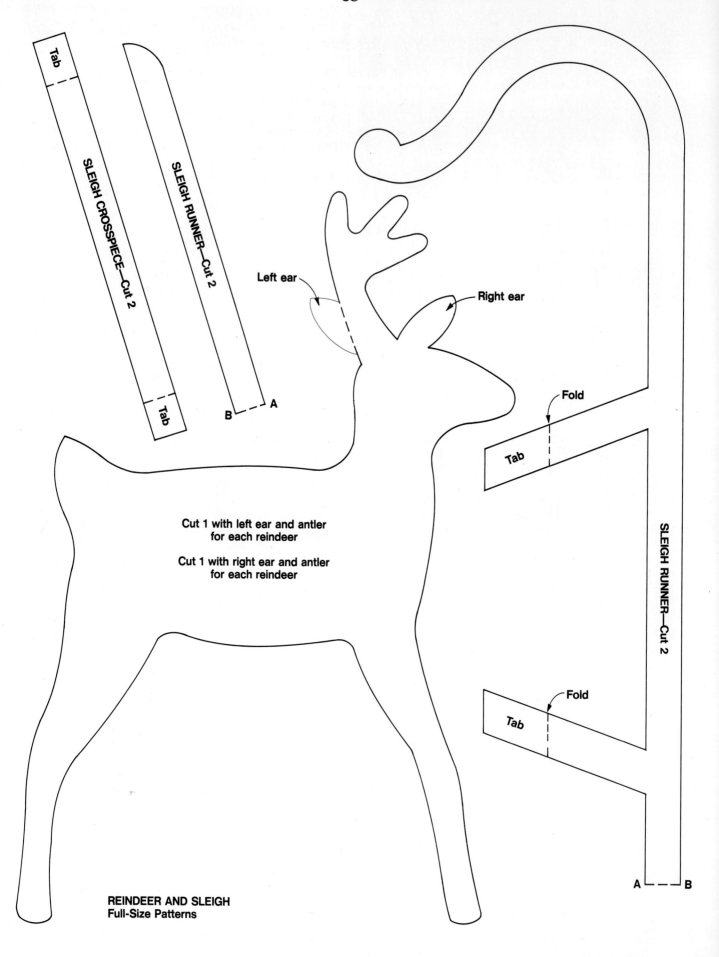

Tab

SLEIGH CROSSPIECE—Cut 2

SLEIGH RUNNER—Cut 2

Tab

Tab

Left ear

Right ear

B — — A

Fold

Tab

Cut 1 with left ear and antler
for each reindeer

Cut 1 with right ear and antler
for each reindeer

SLEIGH RUNNER—Cut 2

Fold

Tab

A — — B

REINDEER AND SLEIGH
Full-Size Patterns

PAPER MERRIMENT

Paper Reindeer And Sleigh

Shown on pages 60 and 61.

Reindeer stand 7¾ inches tall.

MATERIALS
For three reindeer
One 24x36-inch sheet of both chipboard *and* rice paper
Crafts knife
One ½-inch paintbrush for applying varnish
Water-base satin-finish varnish
Quick-dry crafts glue
1 can of flat black spray paint
1 can of flat gray spray paint
½ yard paper crafts cord
¾ yard of ½-inch-wide plaid ribbon; 3 small jingle bells
Purchased wicker wine basket

INSTRUCTIONS
For the centerpiece as shown on pages 60 and 61, make three reindeer. Each reindeer is made from two pieces of chipboard. Two reindeer bodies are glued together, and the legs are spread apart to make the deer stand.

TO MAKE THE DEER: Trace the full-size deer pattern, *opposite,* onto tracing paper. Cut out pattern and draw six deer onto chipboard. Cut three deer, each with a left ear (do not cut the right ear), and three deer with a right ear (do not cut the left ear).

Spray both sides of the deer antlers with gray paint; let dry.

To complete one deer, tear the rice paper into small pieces. Varnish the "right" (front) side on one of the right-eared deer. Fasten small pieces of rice paper to the deer; do not cover the antler. Varnish the paper edges down. When the front side of the deer is covered, varnish the back sides of the legs and fasten rice paper.

Repeat the varnishing and fastening of the rice paper to the companion (left-eared) deer.

Glue the two deer shapes together, wrong sides facing, but leave legs and antlers glue-free. Hold the deer firmly until glue takes hold.

Fasten additional rice paper over the glued seam.

Cut a 6-inch length of crafts cord and place cord around neck, overlapping the ends; glue cord ends together. Let glue dry. Add bow and bell, securing with thin wire or thread. Complete the two remaining deer.

TO MAKE THE SLEIGH: Trace the three sleigh patterns, *opposite. Note:* There are two pattern pieces for the sleigh runner. Join these two pieces at the A–B markings to make one pattern. Cut out the pattern and draw two runners and two crosspiece patterns onto the chipboard; cut out the pieces.

For the base of the sleigh, measure and cut a 3½x3¾-inch rectangle from the chipboard .

Bend the tabs of the runners, and glue the tabs to the edges of the base. Referring to the photo on page 60, bend tabs on the crosspieces and glue these tabs to the runners. Fasten tabs to the inside of the runners.

Spray paint the sleigh runners and base black; let dry. Glue the wine basket to the base.

See page 71 to make the Santa ornament that completes this centerpiece.

Crepe Paper Santa Claus

Shown on page 62.

Santa stands 12 inches tall.

MATERIALS
1½-, 4-, and 5-inch plastic-foam balls
Red and black crepe paper
2½x5¾-inch piece of flesh-colored paper, plus a small piece for the nose
Scrap of gold paper
Empty paper towel tube
2 long pipe cleaners
Cotton batting; 1 cotton ball
Fiberfill; masking tape
12 long straight pins
Black, fine-point felt pen
White crafts glue; hot-glue gun
Powdered rouge or red crayon

INSTRUCTIONS
For the lower part of the body, use a serrated knife to cut away two 3-inch diameter slices from *opposite* sides of the 5-inch ball.

For the upper part of the body, cut away one 2½-inch slice of foam from the 4-inch ball.

Cut a 12-inch square of red crepe paper. Center a flat side of the 5-inch ball on top of the square, and pull the crepe paper up and around the ball. Use hot-glue gun to fasten paper to the flat surface on top, cutting away excess paper to avoid bulk. Pleats will form when pulling paper over ball.

Cut a 12-inch square of red crepe paper, and center the curved side of the 4-inch ball on this square. Pull paper over ball and glue to flat side, forming pleats and trimming away excess paper.

Use the hot-glue gun to glue the two balls together, centering the 2½-inch flat side atop the 3-inch flat side (with the glued end) of the larger ball.

For the lower part of the jacket, cut a 9x22-inch strip of red crepe paper, having the grain of the paper follow the width.

Fold strip in half widthwise so piece measures 4½x22 inches. Cut a ¾-inch-wide strip of batting as long as the paper, and glue it to the folded edge and up each of the short sides of the paper. With a needle and thread, run a gathering stitch across the raw edges. Pin strip around the lower middle half of the 4-inch ball to establish the waist; glue, then remove pins.

Glue a short piece of batting down the center front of the top ball to the edge of the waist jacket. See Assembly Diagram for Standing Santa on page 70.

To make Santa's belt, cut a 3x13½-inch strip of black crepe paper. Fold the strip lengthwise into thirds to make a 1-inch-wide belt. Wrap around Santa's waist, spot glue, overlap ends in front, and glue. Angle-cut the end of the belt. For the belt buckle, cut a 1¼-inch square from the scrap of gold paper. Cut away a ¾-inch
continued

PAPER MERRIMENT

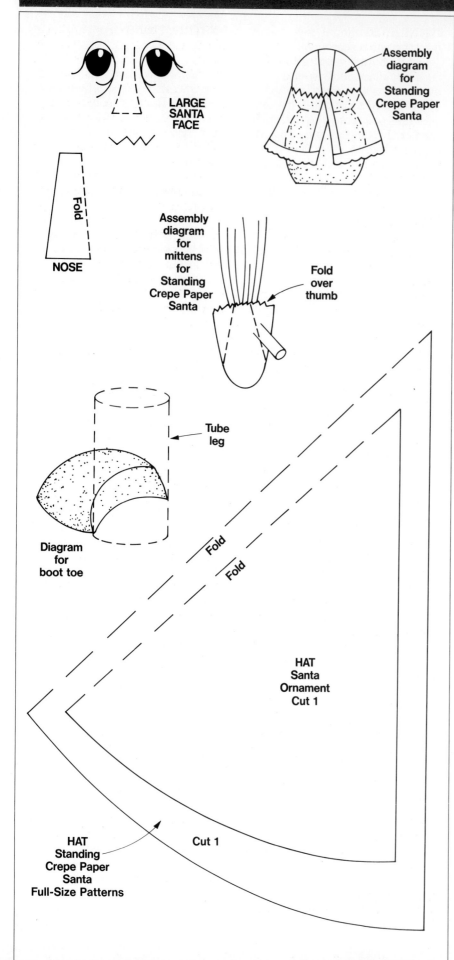

LARGE SANTA FACE

Fold

NOSE

Assembly diagram for Standing Crepe Paper Santa

Assembly diagram for mittens for Standing Crepe Paper Santa

Fold over thumb

Tube leg

Diagram for boot toe

Fold

Fold

HAT Santa Ornament Cut 1

HAT Standing Crepe Paper Santa Full-Size Patterns

Cut 1

square from the center of the 1¼-inch square. Glue buckle to belt.

For the head, cut a piece of paper towel tube 2½ inches long. Using Large Santa Face pattern, *far left,* center and draw the eyes and mouth with felt pen on the piece of flesh-colored paper. Glue paper around the tube. To create his three-dimensional nose, trace nose pattern, *far left.* Cut the nose from the remaining scrap of flesh-colored paper. Glue nose to face at the dashed lines on the face. Color cheeks with rouge or crayon.

Cut the hat from red crepe paper, using larger hat pattern for Standing Crepe Paper Santa, *left.* Hand-sew the long edge together with a narrow seam; turn hat right side out. Glue to top of head, pleating in excess paper.

Cut a ½-inch-wide strip of batting to fit around the bottom edge of the hat, and glue to top of head. Glue cotton ball to end of hat. Fold top of hat to one side and glue in place.

Tape the heads of four straight pins to inside bottom edge of the head tube, spacing them equally. Apply glue to the bottom edge of the tube and along each pin. Stick pins into top of body and push head down flush with the body. Allow glue to dry completely.

For the arms, fold each pipe cleaner in half and then fold in half again. Twist the ends together leaving a 1-inch-long loop at the folded ends for the hand. Cut a 12x5-inch piece of red crepe paper. Gather one piece of crepe paper around the pipe cleaner above the loop, and wrap it with thread to hold it in place.

Repeat the above instructions to make the other arm.

To make the mittens, fold a 1½x4-inch piece of red crepe paper in half widthwise. Roll this up tightly for a thumb; glue the loose edge. Cut a 3x4-inch red crepe paper rectangle, and fold it over the hand loop. Lay the thumb on the back side of the hand, and glue. (See diagram, *above left.*) Fold the excess crepe paper around the back of the hand encasing the thumb in the fold. Wrap with thread around wrist area to hold mitten in place. Cut away any excess crepe paper. Glue a ½-inch-wide strip of batting around wrist to cover the raw edges and thread. Repeat these instructions for the other mitten.

Gather the crepe paper at the top of the arms and glue the arms to the body next to the head.

To make the beard, take a wad of fiberfill, and pull it halfway apart to fit around either side of the head. Attach beard to sides of head and to chin area with glue. Attach a small piece of fiberfill to back of head for hair. Glue wisps of fiberfill over eyes for eyebrows. Wrap a piece of thread around the center of a small piece of fiberfill to make a mustache; glue under nose.

For the boots, cut two 2-inch lengths of paper towel tube. Cut two 3x6-inch strips of black crepe paper. Cover tubes with crepe paper, folding excess paper to insides of tubes.

For the toe of the boot, cut the 1½-inch foam ball in half. From each half, and referring to Boot Toe diagram, *opposite,* cut out a curved section so toe will fit next to boot tube. Cover the toe with a 4-inch square of black crepe paper, gluing the raw edges to the inside edge of the cut curve. Glue toe to the front of the boot tube. Push pins from inside tube into foam to hold toe in place.

To attach boots to the body, tape the heads of four straight pins equally spaced inside top edge of boot, with points extending beyond the tube. Run glue down pins and around top edge of boot. Push pins into bottom flat edge of body until top of boot is flush with body. Allow all glue to dry before moving Santa.

Roly-Poly Santa Ornament

Shown on pages 60 and 63.

Finished ornament is 5½ inches tall.

MATERIALS
3-inch plastic-foam ball
1¼-inch diameter paper towel tube, cut 1½ inches long
One long pipe cleaner
11-inch cord for hanging
4½x1½-inch strip of flesh-colored paper, plus a scrap
Red and black crepe paper
Cotton batting; one cotton ball
Small handful of fiberfill
Black fine-point permanent felt-tip marker
White crafts glue; hot-glue gun
Powdered rouge or red crayon
3 long straight pins

INSTRUCTIONS
For the Santa Ornament, use the same construction methods as for the larger Crepe Paper Santa Claus on page 69.

To make the body (and the base of the jacket), center the foam ball onto a 10-inch square of red crepe paper. Pull the paper around the ball. Use hot-glue gun to fasten paper to the top, cutting away excess paper to avoid bulk. Pleats will form when pulling paper over ball. Trim away the excess paper.

To complete the jacket, cut a strip of red crepe paper 4x18 inches, having the grain of the paper follow the width. Fold strip in half widthwise so piece measures 2x18 inches. Cut a ½x18-inch batting strip. Glue it around the folded edge and up each of the short sides. With a needle and thread, run a gathering stitch around the raw edges. Pull up gathers and pin strip in place around the lower-middle half of the ball to establish the waist of the jacket, and fasten with the white crafts glue. Remove the pins. Glue a short strip of batting down the center front of the ball to the waist. Refer to the assembly diagram for Standing Crepe Paper Santa, *opposite.*

Cut a 1½x11-inch strip of black crepe paper for the belt. Fold paper into thirds widthwise for a ½-inch-wide belt, and glue to waist. Cut a ⅞-inch square of gold paper to make the buckle; cut a ⅜-inch square from its center, and glue to the middle of the belt.

For the head, adapt the Large Santa Face pattern, *opposite,* to fit the flesh-colored paper. Use the felt pen to draw the facial features. Glue the face to the tube. Make the nose from a scrap of flesh paper adapting the nose pattern, *opposite,* and glue to face. Color the cheeks with rouge or crayon.

Use the smaller hat pattern, *opposite,* to make hat from red crepe paper. Hand-sew the long edge with a narrow seam; turn hat right side out. Glue hat to top of head, pleating in excess paper.

Cut a ½-inch-wide strip of batting to fit around the bottom edge of the hat; glue. Cut the cotton ball down to a smaller size and glue to the end of the hat. Fold top of hat to one side and glue.

Tape three straight pins to the inside bottom edge of head tube. Apply glue to the bottom of the tube and along each pin. Stick pins into top of body and push head down flush with the body.

For arms, cut the pipe cleaner in half. For each arm fold each piece in half and make a ⅝-inch-long loop for the hand; twist the ends together. Cut two 2½x5½-inch red crepe paper rectangles for sleeves. Gather one piece of crepe paper around the pipe cleaner above the loop. Secure by wrapping a thread several times around the crepe paper and pipe cleaner. Repeat these instructions for the other arm. Cut batting ½ inch wide for wrist strips and glue in place.

Gather the crepe paper at the top of the arms, and glue to the body next to the head.

Before gluing the fiberfill hair to the back of the head, fold the 11-inch hanging cord in half and knot the ends. Then glue to back of head just under the hat.

To make the beard, take a wad of fiberfill and pull it halfway apart to fit around either side of the head. Attach to sides of head and to chin area with glue. Attach a small piece of fiberfill to the back of the head. Glue wisps of fiberfill above eyes for eyebrows.

6¼- AND 10-INCH SCHERENSCHNITTE TREES
Full-Size Patterns

Fold

Fold

Christmas Tree Scherenschnitte Centerpiece

Shown on page 65.

The three finished trees are 6¼, 8, and 10 inches high.

MATERIALS
3 sheets 8½x11-inch parchment for *each* tree
Tracing paper
Graphite paper
Stapler
Pencil
Sharp 4-inch embroidery or manicure scissors
Sewing needle
Thread to match parchment

INSTRUCTIONS
Select a full-size tree pattern from the designs *opposite* and *right*. Trace the pattern onto tracing paper.

Holding three sheets of parchment together, fold them in half, *lengthwise*. Use the graphite paper to transfer the pattern to the folded papers. Remove the pattern and graphite paper when tracing is complete. Staple the three sheets, outside the traced design area, to hold the sheets in place while you are cutting.

To cut out the design, begin by cutting the areas closest to the fold. Proceed to cut away the inside portions and finally cut away the outside edges.

After the design is cut, unfold the trees; do not take them apart.

Hand-sew the three trees together along the fold line. Space stitches approximately ⅛ inch apart. Open the tree and bend the six halves to form a radiating circle. The tree will stand on its own.

Repeat these instructions for the other tree sizes.

Fold

8-INCH SCHERENSCHNITTE TREE
Full-Size Pattern

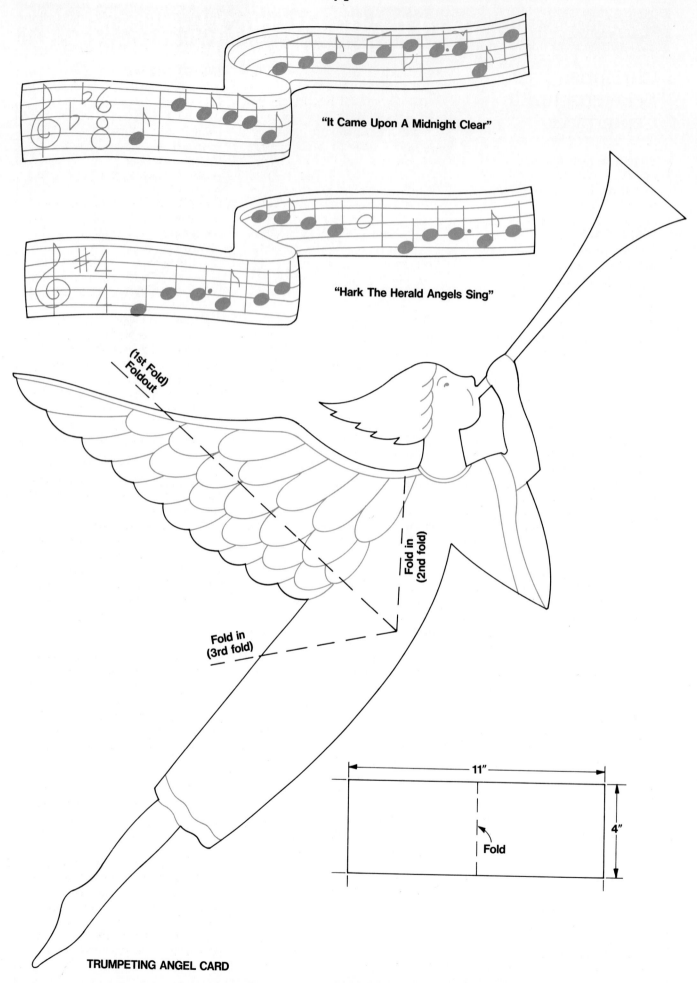

"It Came Upon A Midnight Clear"

"Hark The Herald Angels Sing"

(1st Fold)
Foldout

Fold in
(2nd fold)

Fold in
(3rd fold)

11"

Fold

4"

TRUMPETING ANGEL CARD

Trumpeting Angel Card

Shown on page 64.

Finished card measures 5½x4 inches.

MATERIALS
One 8½x11-inch sheet of rough cover-weight paper, color of your choice
One 8½x11-inch sheet of parchment paper
Fine-line permanent markers
Watercolor pencils
Watercolor brush
Sharp 4-inch embroidery or manicure scissors
Tracing paper
Graphite paper
Pencil
Glue stick

INSTRUCTIONS
Trace the angel pattern and one of the musical score patterns *opposite* onto tracing paper. Trace the fold lines on the angel. Use the graphite paper to transfer the patterns to the parchment; do not trace the fold lines onto the parchment.

Use a fine-line marker to go over the blue lines of the angel and the musical score. Our samples were done using a brown marker.

Decorate the angel with watercolor pencils in colors of your choice, using the photograph on page 64 as a guide. We used a pink pencil to color the leg, face, and arm areas.

Dampen the watercolor brush and go over the colored pencil areas, being careful to stay within the lines.

Lay the paper between several layers of paper towels. Place the paper under a heavy object or book, and let dry.

Carefully cut out the angel and the musical score. Refer to photo on page 64.

Use your tracing pattern and a No. 2 pencil, and lightly mark the fold lines onto the back of the angel; then fold the angel along the markings as shown on the pattern. Follow the folding directions for each step in its numerical sequence as it is shown.

Cut a piece of cover-weight paper into an 11x4-inch rectangle. Fold it in half so that the paper measures 5½x4 inches.

Center the *first* fold of the angel atop the fold of the opened card. Holding the angel in place, glue *only* the trumpet and legs to the card using the glue stick. Make sure that the center folds of the angel and card are aligned before you press the trumpet and legs down to the card. When the card is opened, the angel's wing should pop up.

Glue the musical score across the lower half of the front of the card using the glue stick.

Add your own holiday greeting to the card.

Cross-Stitch Cards and Gift Tags

Shown on pages 66 and 67.

Finished card is 5¼x7¼ inches. The finished gift tag is 3½x2½ inches.

MATERIALS
Ivory perforated paper (available in crafts and needlework stores)
One 10½x7¼-inch piece of card-stock paper in the color of your choice (for one card), one 3½x5-inch piece of card-stock paper (for one tag)
DMC embroidery floss: 1 skein *each* of the following colors: medium Christmas red (304), Christmas red (321), very deep rose (326), rose (335), dark sea foam green (561), sea foam green (562), medium sea foam green (563), topaz (725), dark aquamarine (991), aquamarine (992), white
Gold metallic thread
Tapestry needle
Glue stick

INSTRUCTIONS
Referring to the photo on pages 66 and 67, select the design of your choice. The chart for the "Merry Christmas" card is on page 76, and the chart for the "Christmas Peace" card is on page 77. All the gift tag charts are on page 78.

Locate the center of the design and the center of the perforated paper; begin stitching there. Use two strands of floss to work cross-stitches over one block of the paper. *Note:* It is possible to get more than one design on one piece of perforated paper.

Determine the number of stitches across and down the pattern you've selected to stitch, and outline this area with running stitches. Then allow an additional 4 squares on all sides of this stitching for added paper borders. Determine the center of your stitchery within the outlined area.

BACKSTITCHING: Work all backstitches using one strand of floss or thread.

Work backstitches on the "Merry Christmas" card with dark sea foam green (561). For the "Christmas Peace" card, work the backstitches for the church, snowflakes, pine tree boughs, and pine trees in dark aquamarine (991).

For the gift tags, work backstitches around the holly leaves and pine boughs using dark sea foam green (561). Outline the red candle and red berries with medium Christmas red (304). Use the gold metallic thread to backstitch the outline of the candlewick and flame.

FINISHING: When all the stitching is complete, trim the perforated paper to within 4 stitches beyond the stitched borders. Fold the card-stock paper in half widthwise. Apply the glue stick to the back of the stitched piece, and fasten the piece to the center front of the folded card or tag. Weight the glued card or gift tag down with a book or heavy object until the glue has dried.

CARD

1 Square = 1 Cross-Stitch

COLOR KEY

■ Dark Sea Foam Green (561)　　■ Medium Christmas Red (304)

■ Sea Foam Green (562)　　■ Christmas Red (321)

■ Medium Sea Foam Green (563)　　■ Rose (335)

1 Square = 1 Cross-Stitch

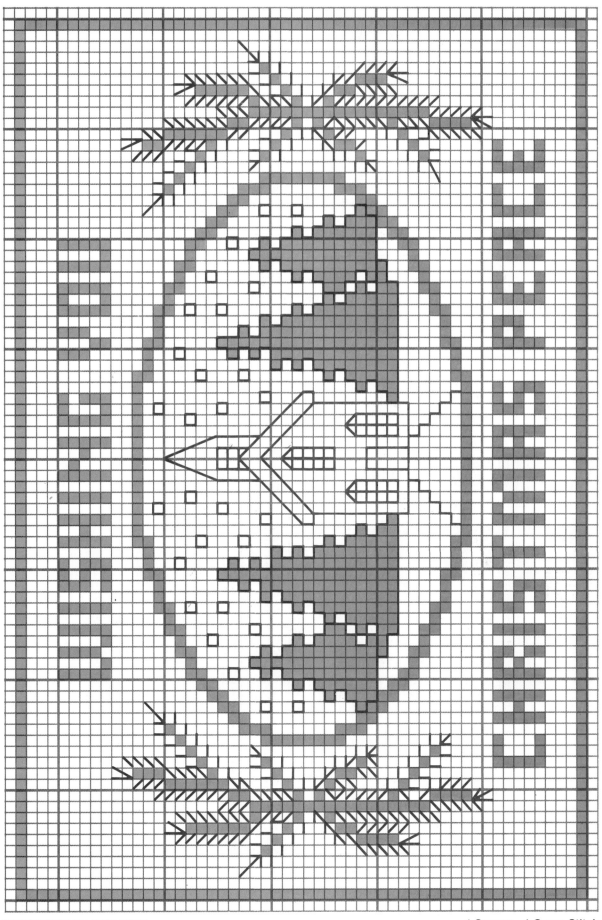

"CHRISTMAS PEACE" CARD

COLOR KEY ■ Aquamarine (992)

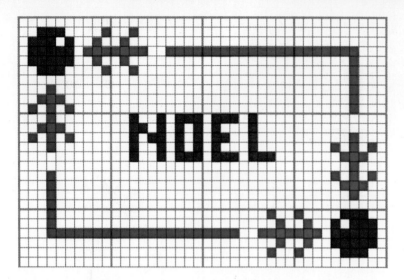

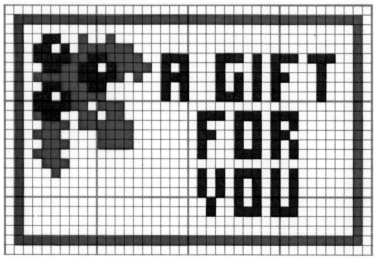

GIFT TAGS   1 Square = 1 Cross-Stitch

COLOR KEY
■ Sea Foam Green (562)   ⊡ White
■ Very Deep Rose (326)   ▨ Topaz (725)

Cut-Paper Snowflake Angel And Tree

Shown on page 67.

Finished angel snowflake is 13 inches in diameter.
Finished tree snowflake is 9 inches in diameter.

MATERIALS
13-inch square of construction, colored tissue, or parchment paper
Sharp 4-inch embroidery scissors
Stapler; teaspoon
Tracing paper
No. 2 lead pencil
White crafts glue
Contrasting background paper or mat board

INSTRUCTIONS
FOLDING THE PAPER PRIOR TO CUTTING: Choose your paper. Thin paper is easier to fold and cut. Refer to the diagrams, *opposite,* for the step-by-step folding instructions.

1 Fold paper square in half diagonally, crease, and unfold.

2 Fold the square in half diagonally in the other direction; leave folded. There is a crease in the center of the triangle.

3 Enlarge the Folding Diagram, *opposite, top,* on a piece of 8½x11-inch paper. Extend all of the lines to the paper's edges. Lay the triangle on top of your diagram, placing the long folded edge atop the horizontal line and the crease on the line perpendicular to the horizontal line.

4 Lift the left corner and crease the paper along the 30-degree line on the left.

5 Lift the right corner and crease the paper along the 30-degree line on the right.

6 Fold the shape in half along the vertical crease in the center of it.

For ease in handling while cutting the motif, staple the layers of paper together along top edges.